A Pennsylvania Mennonite

and the

California Gold Rush

The Journal and Letters
of David Baer Hackman

By Lawrence Knorr

A Pennsylvania Mennonite and the California Gold Rush

REVISED EDITION
Printed in the United States of America
July 2011

Library of Congress Control Number: 2008900705

ISBN 978-1-934597-64-4

Published by:
Sunbury Press
Mechanicsburg, PA
www.sunburypress.com

Mechanicsburg, Pennsylvania   USA

Dedication

This book is dedicated to the memory of my great great uncle David Baer Hackman, all of my extended Hackman relations and to the communities of Lancaster County, PA where they lived and thrived. Oh to have been a fly on the wall in the tavern where David worked – recalling his Gold Rush tales for the clientèle. I am certain there were anecdotes left unwritten.

I would also like to thank the following organizations and persons for their assistance over the years:

The Lancaster County Historical Society for maintaining the original records of the David Hackman story.

The Manheim Historical Society for contributing photos, anecdotes, obituaries and news reports from the era.

The Late Elaine Hackman Grace for all of her work on the Hackman family history.

The Late Emma Hackman White, my grandmother, for being related to such interesting people – and for being one herself.

Preface

This volume is a biography of one of Manheim's more interesting citizens during the latter half of the 19th century. A good bit of this work is comprised of the original letters and journal of David Baer Hackman (above) from the era of his Gold Rush travels. Care is taken to preserve as much as possible the writing style and vernacular of the time and place. An astute reader will notice the improvement of the writer over time.

Additional narratives and explanations are added where necessary to link the events described in the letters and journal, or to provide depth of context or character. Persons, events and places of historical significance are delved into further to provide the reader a better picture of David's contemporaries and the environment in which he was living.

In its entirety, this story tracks the adventure of a young man born to religiously conservative Mennonite stock near Millport, PA as he travels West on the trip of a lifetime. Readers should find this tale an interesting yarn of social history played out during some of the most exciting times of American – even World history.

Chapter 1

The Obituary of David Baer Hackman

David B. Hackman Dead
A Well-Known Citizen Passes Away
He was one of the Pioneers Who Went
to California in Search of Gold –
Engaged in Various Lines of Business,
and For Some Years Followed Shoe making

David B. Hackman, one of Manheim's best-known citizens, died at his home on South Charlotte Street on Tuesday (November 16, 1896) morning about one o'clock. For some time past he had been in ill-health and his illness finally terminated in heart trouble which was the immediate cause of his death. Deceased was sixty-nine years old last March, and is survived by a wife and six children. Mr. Hackman was twice married, a son, Rev. A.M. Hackman, of Lancaster, being by the first wife. The children of the second wife are Frank, telegraph operator and station agent at Marietta Junction, Miss Mabel, Harry, Walter and Edith, all residing at home.

Mr. Hackman became a member of the St. Paul Reformed Church before his death, and the funeral will be held on Thursday afternoon at two o'clock, from his late residence, with services in the church, and interment at Fairview Cemetery. Rev. Chas. E, Wehler will officiate.

Mr. Hackman was born near Clay in this county, and was one of the pioneers who went to California in '49 in search of gold. Most of the distance was traveled on foot. He subsequently returned to this place, bringing some gold dust with him. Afterward, he engaged in various pursuits, having been engaged in the grocery, clothing and hat business, and more recently in shoe making. He was employed by Geo. H. Danner and Co., and John S. Matter, and before compelled by ill-health to retire, he conducted a repairing establishment in the building next to the post office.

Deceased was a member of the Selah Lodge, No. 657, I.O.O.F., of this borough, and enjoyed a wide acquaintanceship in this vicinity. He was a man of kind and genial disposition, and had many friends who will regret to learn of his demise. The family have sympathy of the community in their bereavement.

Mr. Hackman had in his possession at the time of his death some very interesting mementos of his trip to and from California. The letters written are preserved, and give in detail the incidents which occurred in that eventful overland trip which was made from Delaware, Ohio, as the starting point. The return from California, five years later, was made by a circuitous route on land and sea, and the various incidents encountered on that trip are also given in detail. The letters indicate that the writer was a close observer, and what is given is couched in language that shows considerable ability. Mr. Hackman also brought with him some nuggets of gold which are still in possession of the family.

Chapter 2
Farewell My Dear Mother

By the time David Baer Hackman had taken the opportunity to write his mother in Manheim, Pennsylvania concerning his recent life-altering decision to leave work in Delaware, Ohio and head to California, he was already a third of the way on his journey. Perhaps it was the cautious notion of a conscientious son, named after his father who had been lost to the elements as a young man. This 21st day of April, 1850, he was perched by the Missouri River, near the town of Independence, awaiting the opportunity to cross with the wagons. It was his last chance to say goodbye to his mother and expect the letter to be received in a reasonable amount of time. Wrote David:

Missouri River
April 21st, 1850

Dear Beloved Mother,

I will take the pleasure and opportunity of informing you that I am well at present and hope these few lines may find you enjoying the same blessing.

Further, I will inform you that I am a great ways from home. I am on my way to California. I am about two thousand miles from home. I live on the Missouri shore, twelve miles from Independence and three miles from the line of Indian Territory, very near out of the United States. But, then we have to travel twenty-two hundred miles yet by land. We have come by water on to here. We left Cincinnati the 6th of April and arrived on the Missouri shore, opposite Kansas, the 19th of April and we remain here 'til tomorrow. This is Sunday and quite pleasant today.

Further, I will inform you that I am in a company from Delaware, Ohio. There are seventy-five men and fifty horses

3

& wagons and we expect it will take us about three months from here. If we have good luck we can go out sooner. I have seen a good many Indians out here already, but they are as friendly as white men. We expect to meet with some savage Indians, but it is no danger because there are many emigrants traveling to California. You would hardly believe, there are more than thousands and thousands of emigrants going to California. Here is the point where they all come together from all the western states. They are very near all here yet they can't go across the plains 'til the grass comes. I expect, if all put out soon, it will be a train from here half ways to California and I cannot believe it for the sight of people which I have seen. Why, we had on our steamboat over four hundred passengers and about two hundred head of horses, all for California. And so, most all the boats are crowded as much as they can carry.

Food and provisions are very high here and scarce at that. But, we took all our provisions along from home. It cost me or each man about one hundred and sixty-five dollars to go through. We have five men to each wagon and there are seventeen wagons. In the evening we pitch out our tents and make up a great fire and then we stand guard. Every night some of us take turns so as Indians don't take our horses away from us. I am no more discouraged here than I would if I was at home. We cook ourselves in the evening. We set around the fire 'til we get sleepy then lay down and sleep 'til morning. I enjoy myself very well so far.

Dear mother, the object of this communication is to inform you that I thought I would try my luck and see what I can do in California. I have no doubt but what I can do well if I keep my health and live. The prospects are very good of what I have heard. I intend to dig gold if I get out there and if I have good luck, I will be back in course of two years, if I live that long. I will not enclose my letter. I wish you would inform my brother Andrew about this. I did not mean to write to him at present. I wrote him a letter about two months ago and never received answer of him. I don't know the reason why not, but I think it don't make much difference. It's all the same. I did not hear anything from home since last winter. But, I hope you'uns are all alive yet.

Further, if I live and get to California, I shall write a letter back as soon as I know how it is there.

I give my kindest regards to you'uns and to all inquiring friends. Excuse my bad writing and spelling for I had not much time to write.

Remaining yours respectfully,
David B. Hackman

Farewell my Dear Mother. May our prayers meet though we are parted. God grant me a safe journey and a safe return.

Goodbye
David B. Hackman

Mrs. Susannah Brubaker (nee Baer), David's mother, was widowed in 1831, when her first husband, David Heistand Hackman succumbed to pneumonia during a bitter Christmas week that year. According to family legend, he was "half-froze" during a wagon ride from Philadelphia to Sunbury. He was only thirty when he passed, leaving a young wife and three very young children: Jacob (6), David (4), and Andrew (3). According to Orphan's Court records, on April 15th, 1833, these children were assigned to Henry Neslie (Nissley) of Elizabeth Township as guardian. It appears that these boys lived for some time with the Nissleys, developing a strong bond between them.

By the time David Junior was off to the West, his mother had married John Gesell Brubaker, the widower of David Senior's late sister Catherine. This brought together two families of young children. John and Catherine (Hackman) Brubaker had Catherine, Nancy, Henry, Elizabeth, Jacob and Jonas by 1837. John Brubaker and Susannah subsequently added four more Brubakers to the clan – Susan (born 1840), Fanny (1843), Mary (1844) and Isaac (1846). Thus, by the time young David, at age 23, set out for California, he was one of the elder siblings among a gang of 13.

5

David mentioned he was not enclosing a letter to his brother, Andrew (the author's 2nd great grandfather), with his mother's letter. He had begun this letter just prior to his mother's and sent it under separate cover several days later – from St. Joseph's, Missouri. Curiously, it contains a few more details about his decision and experiences en route to Missouri. Additionally, he mentions to his brother that there are two women in the party he is traveling with – a fact he neglects to mention to his mother. It is apparent, from the tone of the letters, that he was much closer to his brother Andrew. Perhaps there had been tension (or lack of attention) between him and his mother as she was now engaged in raising another family of young children with a different man. He seems to tease her with the possibility he will face "savage Indians", but then adds they is "no danger" due to the number of emigrants he is traveling with. David's letter to Andrew reads as follows:

St. Joseph, Missouri
April 21ˢᵗ, 1850

Dear Brother,

I will take the present opportunity, as it may be the last one for some time, to address you with a few lines to inform you I am enjoying good health and am far on my way to California. Little did I think when I left home last fall, that I would be so far out here in the western wilds at this time.

But, it is so. During my sojourn in the state of Ohio last winter, I took the notion like hundreds of others to go to California. So, one day I was traveling along from one place to another, I came to Delaware, Ohio and I learned that a company was organizing to go by overland route to California. I liked the idea of traveling across the plains, so I joined with them. This was the beginning of March, and on the first day of April, they were to go to Cincinnati at which place we would charter a steamboat to take us to St. Louis, Missouri.

There are seventy-three men and two ladies in our company, one the ladies accompanying her husband and the other is a sister-in-law whose husband went to Cala last

6

year. We have seventeen wagons – all new and made to order – and eighty-six horses. We have to take all of our provisions along from here as we cannot get any after leaving this place. Next, we left Delaware (Ohio) on the first day of April as stated above, and as this was the native town of nearly all in the company, except myself, there was considerable shedding of tears on leave-taking. Husbands and wives took leave of each other, children crying, brothers and sisters, lovers and sweethearts all bidding goodbye to each other – all of whom shed copious tears. But finally, like everything else, leave-taking was gone through with, and the long train of wagons started off and soon wives, brothers, sisters and all the dear ones were left far behind, perhaps some of them never to see each other again in this world.

After traveling five days, we reached Cincinnati. Here we had our horses, wagons and all our effects shipped on board the boat - both horses and wagons besides ours – which were also on their way to Cala.

We left Cincinnati on the sixth of April and after a run of fine days, we arrived at St. Louis, Missouri. Here we had to take another boat for St. Joseph. So, after unloading and reloading, we were again under way – which was the second evening of our arrival at St. Louis – April the Twelfth. I enjoyed the trip quite well so far. There was nothing of particular importance transpiring to mar the pleasure of our trip down the Ohio, and up the Mississippi Rivers.

But, in coming to St. Louis, we had some difficulties to contend with. In the first place, the Old Durock, which was the name of the boat, was an old rickety concern, and not fit to travel on. When we came up to Kansas – a small town about twelve miles above Independence – something broke at the machinery of the engine. So the boat was landed at the shore just below town. The captain stated to us that the engine was broke and that he must send it back to St. Louis to get it fixed – which would require about eight or ten days, and during that time he would charge us one dollar and fifty cents boarding per day. So, we told him if he would pay us back our part of our passage money, we would disembark here, but he was wise enough. He said if we would wait till the engine was fixed, he would take us up to St. Joseph.

7

But, the boarding was very poor. In fact, sometimes we had nothing but crackers and coffee, and the idea of paying one dollar and fifty cents per day – we did not like. So, we concluded to disembark and travel by land. We had ourselves ferried across the river here which took one and a half days until horses wagons and everything was across.

This being Saturday, we laid over until Monday, April 20*th*. When we started out, it was about sixty-five miles from here to St. Joseph and a hard road to travel. We had a good many breakdowns. The second day, one wheel broke down. Some had to lay over nearly two days to get it fixed, so we continued on and most every day or two we had a breakdown. At any rate in those sixty-five miles we broke down five times – four wheels and one axletree. Sometimes we stalled – the horses not being used to working together. They got baulky and cut up all kinds of mischief. The country through which we traveled was rather thinly settled, and the greater part through which we came was prairie land. We also met some heavy timber land, in which there were plenty of squirrels. We shot a good many on the way, especially when we had a breakdown – we would go hunting.

Finally, after being on the road ten days, we arrived at St. Joseph, which is situated on the Missouri River about one hundred miles above Independence. There we met hundreds and even thousands of emigrants who came to this place from all parts of the western states, and still they came with their ox, horse and mule teams. The Missourians have principally ox teams from four to six yoked to a wagon.

This was almost enough to give a person the Horace to go to California to see so many people all going to Cala to make their fortunes. But, I am afraid we will be more or less disappointed when we get there. But, as I started to say as I started out, I will see it through if I live and keep my health.

We have to wait here about five days before we can cross the River, on account of so many being ahead of us. There are three ferry boats, two steam and a flat boat. These are busy from morning till night.

We have seen a good many Indians here and on the road, but they area all civilized or friendly to us. But, I *expect to meet with some savage Indians before we get to Cala.*

But, I apprehend not much danger on this account as there will be too many emigrants on the way. It is estimated by some persons here that if all the trains would start out one after the other, there would be a train almost halfway to Cala, and in looking around about the country, and seeing so many camps, and the many steam boats which come in crowded – a person would almost come to that conclusion.

Forage and provision is very high and scarcest that, a great many came here intending to buy their stock or provisions at this place.

We laid in most or nearly all our stock of provisions before we left Ohio. Feed for our horses cannot take along from here as we have not got room on our wagons. Consequently after crossing river at this place we must depend upon grass for subsistence for our horses.

We calculate it will take us about three months to make the trip from here to Cala. The distance they say is about two thousand miles from here. That is a rather long road to travel, through an uncivilized world inhabited only by Indians.

It will cost me about one hundred and sixty dollars and if I have good luck and get my horse through safely, I can sell him and reduce my cost some. Each one has his own horse and some of the men have two. There is from three to five men to each wagon. We are five of us messing together. We have a small sheet iron stove and cooking utensils sufficient for our purpose, and a tent to eat and sleep under. Each wagon is supplied with a tent, stove and etc. because each is a separate mess.

But the whole company is combined so that they must assist each other in case of accidents on the road. We have one in the company who is appointed captain, and one or two to assist him. Therefore, we have to go according to the rules and regulations laid down by him.

We are encamped at present just at the outskirt of the town. Our wagons are all drawn up circle-like, and the tents are put in between.

We do our own cooking and have been doing so since we left the boat because it is cheaper than to board at the tavern – especially here where everything is so very high. They charge as much as five dollars per week for boarding. The town is just literally crowded with people, and all kinds of amusements are going on. I was amused today by seeing a parcel of Indians both old and young shoot at targets with their bows and arrows. Some of the men put five and ten cent pieces on the end of a stick, and some of the little Indians, apparently only five and seven years of age, would let fly their arrows and of the money most every lick, at a distance of about twelve paces. Older ones had to take longer distances as the men would not put up any money at short distances for them because they were a sure shot at incredible long distances.

But, I must bring my letter to close as we got orders to have our wagons and teams at the landing early tomorrow morning – ready to cross over. Everything goes in rotation. We are now four days here. Each company gets a ticket at the ferry office for so many horses and wagons, and when their turn comes, the number of the ticket is called off and if they are not ready the next one is called.

May the Fifth.

This morning we hitched up and drove down to the landing in good style and two of the wagons are already across. So I must hurry up and bring my already lengthy epistle to a close.

When you receive this I will perhaps be far out in the plains, among the Indians and beyond civilization. When I get to California, I will write and give all the particulars of my journey across the plains. Perhaps I have an opportunity to send a letter back with someone, If so, I will.

Hoping this will reach you all in good health, as it leaves me. Give my love to mother and all inquiring friends, and reserve a share for yourself.

Yours Truly,

D.B. Hackman
St. Joseph, Missouri
April 21st, 1850

Chapter 3
To the Edge of the Precipice

In his initial letter home from California, David wrote to his brother Andrew, providing details concerning the crossing of the Plains and the Sierra Nevada. The letter was written over two months after arriving in California, from "Hangtown" (now Placerville).

Hangtown, California
Nov. 7ᵗʰ 1850

Dear Brother,

Having promised you in my last letter to give you all the particulars of my journey across the Plains, I will embrace the present opportunity. After a sojourn of two months in this country, to inform you that after a long and tedious journey of one hundred and twelve days I reached California, nearly wore out, and almost starved to death. I could enter upon a full, and explicit description of all my trials and hardships which I encountered on the way to California. I would merely state that after crossing the Missouri River, we got along tolerable well, until we got within about four or five hundred miles of California, when many of our horses began to fail and some of them had given out entirely. Finally after being en route three months, we reached a place called the Great Meadow (most likely near Lassens Meadow in Nevada), so called on account of the grass that was here. Here we had to make hay to last us to cross the desert, which was sixty or sixty-five miles from there without grass and about forty-five of it without water. But, when we got to this place, there was only two wagons together. Some had lost their horses, and left the wagons back. We had up to this time lost only one of our horses, but two more were giving out. After stopping two days at the meadow, we left in the evening with plenty of

11

hay to travel during night a distance of about 20 miles, to a place called the "Sink" (Humboldt Sink). Here we stopped all day, towards evening we left this place with a few "kegs" of water for our horses as we were now entering upon the desert.

But, we did not get very far during the night, and next day, after the sun got so hot, we laid by till near evening, when we started off again. But by this time our water was all. We did not travel far when one of our horses gave out entirely so we turned him to one side of the road and left him, the road being already lined on each side with dead horses, mules and litter. We had now but three horses to go on with. We got along slowly till about nine o'clock in the evening when we got within about ten miles of the (Carson) River. But our horses could not get along any further with the wagon. So we unhitched them, and I and one of the other men, took the horses to the river. Two of my helpmates stayed with the wagon, till we would return with the horses. After a long and tedious march, we reached the river about midnight, we watered the horses, and gave them some hay, of which we took a small lot along with us. The other wagon which was with us, had better horses than we, and had therefore reached the river sooner than we did with our horses.

After stopping about two hours at the river, giving the horses as much water as they wanted, we were ready to go back for the wagon. As it was not necessary for both of us to go, we drew lots, which of us should go. It happened to be my lot, so I started off again upon my lonely journey. When I got about half-way back, one of my horses began to hang back, and would not go on further. So I left him, and went on with the two, and reached the wagon shortly after sunrise. We had a little hay left. We gave this to the horses, after which we hitched them up, and started on again. When we got where I had left the other horse, he was still there. We took him along. He could then travel again. Shortly after noon we made out to reach the river, but it had not been, perhaps, that the horses knew that they were going toward the water, they could not have held out so long. When they first got water, they could only suck at it. Their tongues were quite stiff and dry.

It was awful to see so many dead horses, mules and cattle laying on this desert, and thousands of dollars worth of wagons, chains, harness, and innumerable other things, all worthless articles, in this part of creation. When we reached the river, we were both out of money and without any provision, and two hundred miles to travel yet.

We could not take the wagon any further, so we dissolved partnership, and each one look out for himself and take along what he could, and the balance leave back. The wagon we traded off, for one pound of flour. There was plenty of provision from here on to California, but flour and ham, or bacon was two dollars a pound. There were some parties who came over here from California with provisions, in order to sell it to the emigrants or trade it on stock, but they could only give from one to five pennies of flour, or "meat" for a horse. After dividing our things, one of my messmates Mr. Kline and I concluded to stay together. But we could not proceed on our journey for a day or two, at least, on account our horses not being in a condition to travel. In the meantime we had to do something to get something to live on. There was no grass within a mile or two of this place, and all the emigrants had to stop here. So on the following morning, Mr. Kline and I went and got out two horses and got the loan of a wagon, and scythe, and went down the river about three miles where we found some grass. We cut as much as we could easily haul, tied it up in sheaves, and hauled to camp. This we sold to the emigrants as they came in from the desert at twenty-five cents a sheave. Before evening we had it all sold. By this operation we made about eight dollars, after paying back four dollars that we had loaned to dinner with. We now had some to get supper and breakfast by living sparingly, but we were used to that kind of living, as we had been on short allowances for several weeks past.

On the next morning, being the third day of our stay here, we went out again for another load. This time we had a job to get a load together, as the grass by this time was pretty much taken up. We made out, however, to get another load to camp as soon after dinner time. This we sold all to one man for seven dollars. We thought now expedient to leave this place as soon as possible as we were told that provisions were cheaper further ahead. Our other men had gone on the day before. One of them had a horse and the other went on foot. Many of our company were back. The two ladies came in on the day before last, we left here. The one whose husband was in California came over and met her here. They both were safe so far.

We packed our things on the horse, which we had the most need of. The balance we left back. We started out from this place in the evening and traveled nearly all night. The horses were again in tolerable good condition. During the night I got lost from the horses, and did not find them till next morning. I got behind the horse on the way. Mr. Kline walked along with the horse and not know whether I was ahead or back. So he traveled on till after midnight when he stopped. I too traveled on until after midnight when I came to where there was a big log fire and two men sleeping alongside. I thought this to be a convenient place, so I laid down on the opposite side and slept till morning. When I got up, my fellow lodgers were up and preparing for some breakfast. After making inquiries in regard to a man and two horses, they told me that a man with two horses turned in here. I took the path pointed to me, and within a few hundred yards where I slept, Mr. Kline had also stopped. We now traveled along for about five days at the end of which we reached out first part of the great Sierra Nevada Mountains, which was about sixty miles across. Provisions along here were only seventy-five cents per pound, but this time we were again out of money and out of provisions. So you may know that we were in rather a bad predicament. We still had our horses, but they would only give us one or two pounds of flour. So we thought to hold onto the horses as long as we could, and trust to chances. We begged sometimes a little flour or crackers. Sometimes we had only three or four spoons full of flour for one meal. This we mixed with water and boiled to a paste, or pap. This we had done for several days, because on the mountain there were no provision stores, or "posts", as they were called. Sometimes we found bones of ham, or pork, which we picked up and ate them off clean. Anything to eat that we found we picked up and ate it. Our horses were bad off as we were. For two nights in succession, they had nothing to eat but oak leaves because on the mountain there was hardly any grass. When we got to the summit of the mountain, we went up on a snow bank which was probably two hundred feet deep. There were two steep places to go up before we got to this one, and one of them was like going up a steep roof. None of those who had good teams could get wagons up this place. On this last mountain top there is a perpetual frost and snow the whole year round. (Most likely the Johnson Cut-Off from Carson City to Placerville.)

But I cannot dwell upon all the trials and hardships that we encountered from the mountain down till we reached the settlements or mines. I would merely say, that since we crossed the Missouri River I have experienced many a hard and toilsome days travel, and may a restless night, accompanied with much suffering both through hunger and thirst, and narrowly escaping of being drowned on several occasions. Recalling to memory all those horrible trials, and sufferings which have accompanied me through the whole length of my journey, are enough to make a person shudder even to think of them. And yet, I did not realize probably at the time, how near upon the "edge" of the precipice I might have stood sometimes.

But thanks be unto Him, who has saved and guided me safely through all these manifold trials and sufferings. But with all these hardships I did not feel despondent or even wish and desire to be back in the old "Keystone State". My only wish and desire was to reach California. I was very often so fatigued and tired out, that I could lay myself down upon the ground and sand to rest and sleep in oblivion of being left behind. But there was no cessation until at the end of my journey, which finally terminated on the twenty-third day of August A.D. 1850.

Having crossed the Missouri River on the fifth of May and arriving on the twenty-third of August, being therefore one hundred and twelve days in crossing the Plains, a distance of about two thousand miles. And during this long trip, we had a considerable sprinkle of snow, hail and rain storms and a few tornadoes and besides this having traveled over hills and mountains and through almost endless valleys, across creeks, and large rivers, and long desert places which were both hot and dry.

15

And finally we came to that stupendous mountain the "Sierravada". Out of a warm and pleasant valley we ascended until we reached an elevation of perpetual frost and snow, from whence we again descended until we reached a corresponding latitude from that of the opposite side of the mountain, but of a more healthy and beautiful climate.

So here I am in the land of Cala among strangers and in a strange land.

But whether my sojourn in California will be attended with as many ups and downs, as has been my journey across the plains, is a question undefinable to me. But I hope, however, that it may be to the contrary.

We arrived at the first settlement in the evening with not a cent of money, or a mouthful to eat. Next morning we sold our horses for sixty dollars, which was as much as we could reasonably expect, considering the low condition in which they were.

We divided the money. Mr. Kline now left me and went to Sacramento City, about sixty miles from here. While I went to Hangtown about three miles north from where I first landed. I have not been digging much gold yet. I worked around a little and get about as much as it cost me for my "Grub" which is not less then about a dollar pay. Provision is very high. Flour is twenty-five cents per pound, Pork twenty-five to thirty cents per pound, ham hock fifty cents, twenty-five cents with rice, twenty-five with sugar fat back, with coffee one dollar per pound, tea $1.70 per pound, molasses one dollar per quart, potatoes twenty-four to thirty per pound, onions one dollar per pound and everything else in proportion. I housed myself because I can do it for nearly half what it would cost me at a boarding house, where they charge from twelve to fifteen dollars for a week. I have not done much mining as I stated but I am satisfied that there is plenty of gold here. Some are making from five to ten and as much as a hundred dollars per day, but they are few who make that much.

Perhaps when I am here awhile I can then tell you more about the gold mines. I am all by myself. There are some of our company stopping here too. They got all through as far as I know, but one man died on the plains.

In my next letter I will give you a full description of California as far as I have seen it, and of the summer and winter seasons, which they say is about five or six months raining, and the balance dry. It is now near the time when the rainy season commences. I will now bring my letter to close, stating however that I am enjoying good health, at present. The first week of my arrival I was not so well. I was eating too much at first, which was the cause of rather bad results. It took about four weeks before I could satisfy my hunger. If I was eating ever so much, I was still hungry. But now I am alright again and getting fat.

Please give me all the news from home as I am very anxious to hear from you all. I have no news from home since I left the States. There is no post office here yet, so direct your letter to Sacramento City, California. My respects to all inquiring friends.

Yours truly

D.B. Hackman

Chapter 4
A Description of Crossing the Desert

David had also recorded the details of this journey in his journal:

It was in the month of August in 1850 that we arrived after a long and tedious journey of three months en route for California. At a point, on the Humboldt River, called the Great Meadow, this is a general stopping place for the emigrants, to recruit their stock, and also to prepare themselves with a good supply of hay for the desert. The distance from this point across the Desert was sixty miles without grass and forty-five miles without grass or water. We left the Meadow in the evening with a good supply of hay and traveled to a place called the sink (Humboldt Sink). The water sinks away here between this point and the Meadow. The river is formed into a large lake. Below this place it runs through quite a deep and narrow channel, where it finally sinks away altogether. We left this point at the afternoon with as much (two lines omitted)
...we intended to cross the desert during the night on account of getting through before it is getting so hot the following day. But we missed it, as you will soon see. In following down the channel several miles, we came to where the road crosses the stream. This we found too difficult to cross on account of our horses being too weak. It was cut up so much by the large emigration that passed over before us. What is became a perfect mire; after seeing some cross over, we concluded not to risk our teams but proceed farther down the stream in hopes of finding a better crossing. But instead of finding it better, it got worse. The channel got to be so narrow and deep that it was almost impossible to cross on any account. But night was overtaking and to return back was too far, and to proceed further down was out of the question on account of the hills. After a short consultation, however, we hit upon a plan; we

must unhitch our team and unload the wagons. There was one other way besides ours and several packers on horseback. After we had everything unloaded we were then ready for a general splash. One horse after other was then hauled down over the bank. The opposite side wasn't so steep and therefore better to get out and only about six feet across. The luggage we had to carry over on our heads on account of the water being too deep to carry it on our shoulders. Lastly came the wagons. These we drew over by means of ropes, one tied on behind to keep the wagon from tipping over in going down the bank. After considerable labor, however, we got everything safely across. But by the time that we were ready to start again, it was near twelve o'clock. Thereby we lost much time in taking a new route, so much so that by morning, we had not come much more than seven miles from the point of which we started from the afternoon previous. During the (line omitted)...

...the heat towards evening we traveled again. But we were already too long on the desert. Our Horses were declining very fast. Two out of the four in our mess were about giving out. The hot and sandy Desert and the insufficiency of water is very hard on stock. The water used in crossing the desert is very much impregnated with alkali, which is the cause of so much stock dying in crossing the desert. The road is lined on either side with dead horses, cattle, mules, wagons, chains, iron of every description strewn along the road—all useless articles in that part of the country. At about ten o'clock in the evening on the second day, we got within ten miles of Carson River. Our nearest point to water, being out so long already, we got short of water and our horses were about giving out. One of them we had left already. We had now but three Horses to go on with and these could not draw the wagon through the deep sand.

We therefore obliged to unhitch and leave the wagon for the present. Two of us accordingly started off with the horses for the river while the other two of our messmates stayed in regard to getting our horses through even without the wagon. Notwithstanding their apparent weakness, however, after a long and tiresome ride, we made out to reach the river, a large and fine stream, the best water that we had met for many a days travel. Here we watered our horses and gave them some hay of which we had a small supply with us. After stopping a sufficient length of time to water and rest the horses, it got to be about three o'clock in the morning, we were then ready to return for the wagon. But we thought it not necessary for both of us to return with the horses. Therefore, we cast lots to see which of us should go. It happened to be my lot. I therefore started off with the horses considerably refreshed. On my way out, I met with teams every now and then, and a driver on each side, whipping and striking continually, as though they would strike new life into the poor animals. It is dreadful to see the things that will come to view in crossing the desert. It is no pleasing thing to be on the desert without a companion, especially after night, when you see dead objects on either side of the road and many still are struggling between life and death. Some are cutting deep holes into the sand, in trying to get up. What made it more dismal still was the howling of the wolves and barking of the prairie dogs. They would sometimes strike up a chorus that would sometimes make a persons hair stand on end.

After traveling along at the slow rate of about three miles per hour, I had come about six miles when one of my horses felt rather indisposed to go any further. He knew, perhaps, that he is going away from the water. At any rate, he would not travel. So, I turned him on one side of the road, and left him. I had now but two horses to fetch the wagon and this was rather a doubtful cause. But I went on with the two horses. I reached the wagon at about eight o'clock in the morning. My companions were anxiously awaiting my return. We then gave the horses hay as much as they would eat. At about ten o'clock AM, we concluded to hitch up and take the wagon as far as we could. We accordingly started off. On our return, we met the other horse on the very spot where I had left him. So, we took him along. He could travel again. We traveled along slowly until some time in the afternoon. We made it out to reach the river once more. Had it not been that the horses knew that they were going towards the water, they would not have held out as long as they did. They were nearly exhausted that when we first offered them water, they could only suck at it. But they soon *revived again. We then took them down the river about a mile where there was good pasture. Here we left them for a few days, among other horses, in order to give them a good rest and also to make some preparations for packing. As we could not take our wagon, we sold it for one pound of flour. At this point of the river, there was quite a large camp. All the emigrants made this their stopping place for a few days. There are very few who can continue on their journey after crossing the desert because there is another distance of twenty-five miles ahead without grass. It is therefore necessary for the emigrants to stop at this point of the river in order to give their stock sufficient time to regain their lost strength.*

Chapter 5
Description of Our Sojourn at Carson River

The day following of our arrival at the river, we concluded that each had better shift (port or carry) for himself, as we had no wagon anymore. We accordingly divided what things we had, which by the by, was nothing but cooking utensils and some other little fixings. We had neither money nor provisions after arriving here. This was rather a hard case, especially as we had two hundred miles to travel yet. Provisions, however, were plenty from here to California, as there were plenty of traders who came over from the latter place to meet the emigrants with the intention of exchanging their provisions for stock at enormously high prices. They would offer from one to five pounds of flour or bacon for a horse or a mule. The above articles were readily sold at two dollars per pound, and other things in proportion. It was therefore not very profitable to stop here long. However it made no difference with us, as we had no money nothing but the three Horses left among the four of us and those were individual stock. Three of us therefore had horses whereas the one who lost his had none. After our division, however, I and one of my messmates, whom I will call Dan, concluded to stay together as each had a horse. We also made an offer to the man without a horse to take him along, providing he would reduce the weight of his baggage to be equal with that of ours. He had about a hundred weight, while both of us had only about thirty-five pounds. To this he would not agree. He accordingly left us with the whole of his baggage on his back. The other Man who had a horse left too. So, me and Dan were now left to pursue our own course as best we could. But we could not resume our journey for a day or two yet on account of our horses not being in a traveling condition. Meanwhile, we must do something for ourselves in order to get provisions. There was but one chance of doing this we could see and that was by cutting grass and selling it to the emigrants as they came in from the desert as there was no grass to be

22

had within two or three miles of this place. They most generally wanted a little previous to watering their stock, and very frequently some would come in from the desert with part of their teams only while some of them could not get along anymore. They would then buy a few sheaves of grass and take it out on the desert to meet their exhausted stock. By taking grass and water they can sometimes bring in such stock as there were some in the grass business. We thought to try it too. We accordingly went to get our horses, and wagon, or rather the wagon that we had owned, and a scythe, and started off down the river about three miles where we found a good spot of Grass. There, we cut and tied it up in sheaves, as much as we could haul with two horses. After having as much as we could take, we started off again, and got back to camp by noon. This was on the second day of our sojourn at the river. During the afternoon we had the good fortune to dispose of all the grass that we had, at twenty-five cents a sheaf. By this speculation we gained about eight dollars. This was scarcely enough to buy dinner and supper with, after paying back five dollars that we had the loan of, to get the dinner with, for which it cost us four dollars, and only had one pound of flour, and one of bacon. However we made out to get supper for the balance of the eight dollars and had a little left for breakfast the following morning, not without living very sparingly. But we were used to this as we had been on short allowance for the last two weeks previous.

The next day brought us another load. But this we could not dispose of so readily, as the grass market was tolerably well-stocked by this time. During the day however, we disposed of this load. We now thought it expedient to leave this place as soon as possible on account of provisions being cheaper further ahead. We accordingly went to work and packed our things. By six o'clock in the evening we were ready to resume our journey once more with but seven dollars in our pockets. The reason of our leaving at this time of day was in order to reach, during the night, a certain place where there was water and grass some twelve miles ahead from whence there was another desert of twenty-five miles. After leaving camp, we traveled along briskly as our horses had nothing to carry but our little clothing and we

23

were again in tolerably good order. We walked along briskly until after dark, when we came to where there was a trading post, so called because they had provisions for sale. Here I stopped in to ask the prices of provisions, while my companion was going on with the horses. I had stopped perhaps fifteen minutes when I started off again with the intention of soon catching up with the horses. But in this I was disappointed. I walked about two miles when I came to where there were two roads. One of them was the main road while the other was turning off to the left to where there was kind of a camp and trading post. Here I was at a loss which of the two to take. However, I kept the main road, and started to run for about two miles further, when I thought he could not have come so far yet. So I sat down alongside the road to await his appearance. I thought he had taken the road leading to the above named trading post, and perhaps was stopping there all night, so I started back to see if he was there. But not finding him here, I concluded he must be ahead after all. I therefore started off again and walked till about midnight when I came to where was a big log fire and two men laying alongside asleep. I was tired out considerably and thought this a convenient place to take up my night quarters so I slid down alongside the fire to sleep till morning without anything to cover myself and but the root of a tree for a pillow.

Next morning when I awoke, I found my fellow lodgers up and preparing for breakfast. After making some inquiries in regard to my horses and companion, they informed me that there was a man with two horses who turned in here and they showed me a road or trail which led off from the main road. I accordingly took the direction which they pointed out to me, but I had no intention of going far. Within three hundred yards from where I slept, I found my companion just getting up. I might have seen him from where I was, had it not been for the low marshy place full of willows and bushes in between us.

My companion did not know what to think of my disappearance. He thought I was on ahead so he kept on with the expectation of catching up with me until he came to where the Log fire was. Here he concluded to stop for the night. He accordingly turned in here to find a suitable *camping Place. In this respect both had the same idea for stopping at one place. I thought it best to keep up with the horses after this then I won't get lost. After we had been having a short discourse in regard to our nights adventures, I asked him where he had the Horses. He said he turned them out after unpacking them. So I went to look for the horses while he was preparing breakfast. I found them close by. One of them was in a predicament not easily to be get out. He was mired down. So I called my companion to help me draw him out. This was a rather difficult job, after considerable labor. However we got him out on dry land. This was a matter of no great importance to us as it was the case very often on our journey hither ward. After seeing that our horses were all right for the present, we went to get our breakfast, which was done up in a frugal manner.*

After having disposed of out breakfast, we packed up our things and started out again. We now traveled along tolerable well for about three days without anything worth noting down. At the end of this time, we reached Carson Valley. Here we had plenty of grass and water, of which our horses stood very much in need of, as the grass was very scarce for the last three days travel. We thought it necessary to travel very slow, as long as we are in the valley, in order to have our horses in a good condition for crossing the Sierra Nevada Mountains, to which mountains we had yet about sixty miles. We had still a little money left, by living very economically. Flour and bacon got down to seventy-five cents per pound along here. After traveling along slowly for three days more, we came to the mountain. Here we found ourselves in a fine meadow among numerous other emigrants bound in on all sides except on the east and southeast by the mountain whose snowy peaks showed themselves high above our heads. In taking a view of the mountain, it appeared almost impossible to find a passage through it. But there evidently be one, as the emigrants are all moving towards the mountain as though they would go through underneath. However we will see when we get there. After stopping a day and night at this meadow, like many others as previous to entering the mountain gorge or canyon, we proceeded on our journey. But by this time we were out of money and provisions again, and were therefore wholly dependent upon those who would gratify us with a little bread stuff as we go along from one trading post to another.

Chapter 6
Crossing the Sierra Nevada

Beg our way through as it was, but we could not help that, even though we had our horses to dispose of. Yet they would only offer one or two pound of flour or hard bread, for one, so we thought best to hold onto the horses and see our way through as best we could, which was on a small scale enough, especially when we used but four spoonful of flour mixed up with water and boiled besides coffee to serve for one meal. We have done that for several days and by all this we did not despair once. We felt about as happy as could be expected under the circumstances that we were in. But to resume our journey after leaving the meadow as aforesaid, we traveled along for a mile or so. We came to a river—the head water of the Carson River. This stream came down a steep canyon as it is called. This we followed along up for about eight miles when we came to what appeared to be a level country, heavily timbered, and pasture very scarce. The climate was much colder then it had been previous to coming on the Mountain. We now traveled along for a day and a half at the end of which time we came to another rise in the mountain. This was impassible for wagons. None but those that have strong teams could get their wagons up. It appeared like going up a steep roof, distance about a quarter of mile.

That was one of the places that rode off where they hitch fourteen yoke of oxen to one wagon. It is as much as a horse can do to walk up, let alone draw anything. Some get their wagons part of the way up then left them as they could not get along. Even though they get them up the steepest part, there was still a distance of about three quarters of a mile to reach the summit which was more obstructive than the steeper part, on account of the road being so very narrow and rocky. I noticed one particular place about halfway up where they had to take the wagons apart to get them through between the rocks just wide enough for a horse or mule to walk through. Many of the emigrants had to leave their Wagons here. It was so full of wagons and so little room that, in order to clear the road, they had to pile the wagons on top of one another, which was actually the case here. It was one of the greatest places, I presume, that men ever undertook to go over with wagons. It was a perfect mass of rocks on each side of road. After passing this place and winding though the mountain, we soon reached the top. Here we stopped to noon or rather to rest—both ourselves and horses, as neither we nor the horses had anything to eat of any account.

It was here just like early spring. The snow was not all gone yet, and therefore not much grass for our horses. From this place we had a fine view of the snowy mountain, which was not many miles ahead of us. After stopping a couple of hours, we again resumed our journey. We traveled along slowly over hills and through valleys till nightfall when we reached the foot of the great snow mountain with two other men who fell in with us a few days previous. The grass was no better here than it had been our last stopping place.

After unpacking our horses, we went to work to build up a large fire in order to cook a little coffee, and also to warm ourselves by as the nights got to be quite cold along here. We had some trouble of finding water here, as it was dark when we stopped. But after walking around considerably among rocks and bushes, we had satisfaction to find enough springing out of the rocks to get supper with.

Next morning, after daylight made its appearance, we went to look for something to eat for our horses. We found a little grass among the rocks, where we left them for a few hours. It was now proposed that two of the company should take their guns and go in pursuit of some game during the day. Accordingly, my companion and one of the others started off after Breakfast while I and the other one brought the horses along. Each of them had a horse and were no better off with provisions than we were. It was agreed that the hunters should strike the road somewhere ahead of us, an hour or so after they were gone. Me and my fellow companion packed up and started off. We now traveled along on the ascent for about a mile and half, when we came to a large hollow on the mountain of trees or bushes.

After crossing this we came onto a perfect snowbank, and very steep going up for about half a mile. If it had not been for the snow there, it would perhaps be impossible to get up. But there is perhaps fifty or a hundred foot of snow, which makes it more gradual in coming up on the side of the mountain. It was very difficult in going up as it was so smooth and our horses not being roughshod. It is no easy matter for those that have wagons to cross over this bank of snow as it is steep off on one side and makes it therefore dangerous to upset and go down over the snowbank, in which case it would be needless in trying to get a wagon out anymore.

At about eleven o'clock AM we reached the summit, this was the highest and last rise in crossing the mountain. This place can be plainly seen from Sacramento City which is a hundred miles distant from here. I tried to look down to see the settlements of California, as I was told that they could be seen, but there was nothing to be seen westward from here, except that which appeared to be the sky.

After stopping an hour or so to rest, and to see all that we could see, we started down the mountain which was quite steep for a short distance. We traveled for several miles when we came to a halt to take our nooning. The grass along here was somewhat better than what it had been on the east side of the mountain. Our hunters had not yet made their appearance. We were in hopes of having some game for dinner, but instead of that I had to content myself with coffee and a little hand bread.

We traveled on during the afternoon with the expectation of meeting them on the road. But night came and still no hunters. So we encamped for the night all by ourselves, that is two of us only, among the tall pine trees of which there are oceans of them. I had a very scant supper and no prospect for any breakfast except coffee of which article we had a small supply yet. But morning came and still we were alone, so I made myself a strong cup of coffee which was all I had for breakfast. We were now at a loss whether to proceed on our journey, or to wait for our companions. After waiting awhile and making some inquiries of those who passed, without receiving any tidings, we put up a notice with our names thereon, and proceeded on our journey.

29

After traveling till bib we cane to a trading post. Here we found them in rather a fatigued condition as they had been out the whole day and night previous, and had had nothing to eat but a few birds which they happened to come across during their rambles through the mountain.

We now traveled along for about three days during which time both ourselves and horses lived on very short allowance. We had to feed our horses on oak leaves for two nights in succession, as we were traveling on the ridge of the mountain where there was no grass to be had of any account.

At the end of the three days we came to a place where some traders had a large stock of hay, which they sold to emigrants at fifteen cents per pound. But we had no money and could not buy any for our horses. This hay was made previous to coming in of the emigrants, some two miles from the road, where there was a meadow of about fifty acres. We took our horses there but we found not much grass as it was cropped short and dried up.

We left our horses here for an hour or so to pick what little they could find, after which time we returned to the road where we met with an old acquaintance of ours, one who had been in company with us in the fore part of our journey. After the usual compliments were passed, he inquired of us, why we don't stop at some place and receive recruit of our horses, as he saw they were in awful condition. But our telling him of the circumstances that we were in he reached in his pocket and drew out two dollars and gave it to us with the words that if we ever see him again and have the money we should refund it, and if not we were welcome to it. Of course we thanked him for his kindness. We then went to a trading post close by, and purchased two pounds of flour and a pound of pork at half a dollar per pound each. This gave us a good afternoon meal and saved a little for next day.

We had twenty miles yet to the first settlements, which we hoped to reach the next day. We traveled a short distance during the afternoon and evening, but our horses could not go far at a time. After traveling till dark, we had perhaps some five miles. We stopped for the night and unpacked our horses and lead them down a steep mountain into a valley, where we left them to fend for themselves, not knowing whether or not we should ever see them again.

We were again left by ourselves here as our former companions had better horses than we had, and could therefore travel faster than we did. They were therefore ahead of us. As soon as it was light enough on the following morning, I started off in quest of the horses. Meanwhile my companion prepared breakfast. In the course of two hours I returned with the horses. I found them at least two miles off from where we turned them out and they were somewhat refreshed.

Chapter 7
Among Strangers and in a Strange Land

After breakfast, we again resumed our onward course, which we hoped to be our last days journey if nothing should happen to prevent us from traveling. After trudging along till nearly night, we came within four miles of Ringgold which was the first town that we would strike on our road. (Ringgold was in El Dorado County, California. It was the first settlement along the Carson Pass, possibly named after Cadwalader Ringgold of the 1841 Wilkes Expedition.)

We had fifty cents left yet of the two dollars which we received the day previous. This we laid out for flour to get supper with before entering town. We got for our fifty cents half a pound of flour and the same quantity of pork, which we mixed up to the best advantage. After supper, we again started off and at about nine o'clock we reached the little city of Ringgold, without a cent of money or a mouthful to eat, among strangers and in a strange land. Thus we reached the long-sought for destination, being en route one hundred and twelve days.

After arriving in town, we stopped before a hotel as it was termed. But it might properly been called a gambling house, as gambling was carried on to the highest degree. Here we found ourselves in the midst of a busy world, composed of gamblers, miners, traders and scores of emigrants, all seemingly happy with the one great object before them which was to make their "piles" in a short time and then to return again to their far distant homes.

After stopping a little while and consulting how to proceed now, we were about to move outside of the town to take up our night quarters in a remote place, where we wouldn't be disturbed by the noise and confusion that was occasioned in town, when we were accosted by a man who made inquiries concerning some teams that he was expecting in from the mountains that he came in ahead of them and wished to know whether we had seen them.

Whereupon we informed him in the negative, but meanwhile we knew that his object was merely to get into our graces in order to buy our horses. Nevertheless, he was a generous man, for after finding out the circumstances that we were in, he offered to get supper for us or anything that we wished to have. After thanking and telling him that we don't wish anymore as we had had supper, he said we should come here in the morning when he would give us the loan of as much money as we need till we can dispose of our horses. Accordingly we parted for the night, he taking up his nights quarters in a shanty or some other place, while we went out on the side of a hill to take up our quarters. Here we unpacked and turned the horses out to pick up what little they could find, for grass there was none. At this season of the year everything dry, no rain from early spring until fall. On the following morning after having a tolerable good nights rest, we were up and doing. I went to see the horses while my companion went to see our new friend. After walking around considerably I found them and brought them towards town, where I left them till after breakfast, if we should have the luck to get any previous to selling the horses. However, I was apprised of the agreeable fact when coming in sight of our camp, to see a bright fire, and my companion busy in preparing breakfast. After leaving my companion, he went to town where he found our friend who advanced money enough to get breakfast with, of which we parted with a raving appetite.

Chapter 8
Dear Miss Miller

David wrote to his romantic interest, Harriet Miller who lived in Manheim, Lancaster County, Pennsylvania.

Hangtown, Upper California
November 8th 1850

Dear Miss,

I will take the present opportunity of informing you that I am well at present, and hope these few lines may reach you enjoying the same state of health. Further I will inform you that I reached California August the twenty-fifth. It took us one hundred and twelve days to come across the plains. That was a long and hard trip. It is hard enough to kill anybody but I stood it very well. Till I got here, I felt unwell for a week or so. But now I am well and as fat as ever improving every day.

I will inform you that I expect a letter of you before this time. I have been looking for a letter ever since I have been here and all in vain. But I want you to write to me as soon as you receive this letter. I would very much like to hear from you because I ain't heard from you for six month and it will be two month longer yet before I get to hear of you and that is rather long not to hear of a dear love which it use to be. But whether it is so now or not that I don't no. But I hope it may be so yet.

Dear Miss, I will not write much more this time. I have wrote to you last and you know all about what I did write, and now I want you to write as soon as possible if you please, and write to me whatever you think proper and I will answer you. I will inform you that I don't expect to leave California till this winter a year then I come home if I live and keep my health.

Now don't neglect and write to me. Excuse me for not writing more. I mean to write more the next time – if I receive an answer of you.

I will send you a specimen of the California gold.

Excuse my bad writing and spelling because we ain't got so convenient a place to write and or set on. We ain't got chairs to set on nor tables to write on. A person is deprived from everything here which he don't know when he is to home. I will close my letter now.

Direct your letter to Sacramento City
Your humble servt

David B. Hackman

Chapter 9
Hangin' in Hangtown

Christmas in Hangtown (now Placerville), California, David is alone but reflecting upon his life as a prospector. He writes his brother Andrew concerning the activities in the town and nearby mines.

Early drawing of "Hangtown", circa 1850.

Hangtown, California
Dec. 25ᵗʰ 1850

Dear Brother,

As I do not expect an answer on my last letter for a month or six weeks as it takes at least three months for a letter to go and come because the mail facilities are not being good yet, between this Country, and the states. Therefore, I will embrace the present opportunity to write another letter in the interval. Today is Christmas, but it don't look like Christmas because we have no roast turkey, nor boiled chicken, or anything of the kind, and the weather is anything but Christmas weather. You would be surprised if you could just step over here for a day or so and see the beautiful weather that we have had all this fall. They say there is hardly ever any snow falling here, but a little higher up on the mountains there is snow falling still during winter.

Contrary to expectations, the rainy season has not yet set in and there is not the least appearance for it at present. We had but two little showers, and one by one, which was also unlooked for, because it was quite before the time when it usually commences to rain.

That was in September about six weeks after I got to this country and I had about as good a ducking then as was necessary, for a poor houseless miner as I then was. I had been camping in company with two of my fellow miners in a brush shanty at the time, and as I had not as yet concluded upon my winter quarters, not knowing whether I would stay in this neighborhood or nor, and deeming the time sufficiently long enough to provide for that, before the rainy season would set in, consequently I was left houseless like hundreds of other fellow miners. During the afternoon, threatening clouds came up accompanied with heavy thunder and just about night fall, the rain came pouring down in torrents. I had just been preparing a savory dish of beefsteak and had it yet on the fire when it commenced raining. My fellow campers had had their supper and were already gone in quest of a better shelter place. But I was not to be cheated out of my supper in this manner, so I stood the ground until I had finished my meal. But before I was though with it, I had nearly half a dish full of gravy added to that which I had made. After which I went about to look for more comfortable quarters, it had got to be quite dark by this time. After considerable trouble, I made out to get shelter in an unfinished frame shanty, which was just being roofed over that day. This, however, was crowded to excess. But I forced my way inside of it where I had to maintain an upright position until after the rain was over, which kept pouring down until long after Midnight, after which we again dispersed, but everything being wet we did not sleep

*any that night. Next morning it was again bright and clear
and not a cloud to be seen.*

*Nevertheless a great excitement was now prevailing
among the hundreds of houseless miners. I say hundreds,
because there were hundreds within a circumference of less
then half a mile. The prevailing excitement on this occasion
was that the rainy season would shortly be at hand.*

*Therefore something had to be done in order to fortify
ourselves against another ducking. The consequence was
that shanties were erected by the hundred in a very short
space of time. I and two other men went to work and put up
a shanty. We went up on the hills where there was plenty of
pine trees. We cut some poles set them in the ground one to
each corner and some in the middle, split some clapboard to
shut up the sides, and roof, and build a chimney at one end,
no floor in this. We were done in less than a week. We had
to work very had. We carried everything. Some poles we
carried more than a mile from off the hills. You will perceive
by this that life in California is not a very pleasant life. We
have not the comforts of home life here, like you have there.
You have a good soft bed to sleep in and a table to set down
to eat off of. While we eat and sleep on the ground. But I am
used to this kind of life and I feel not the least discouraged
about it so far.*

*I will also tell you something about Hangtown. This you
will say a queer name for a town, but it derived this
appellation from the fact that three men were hung at one
time here, about a year ago, since which time it is called
Hangtown.*

*This reminds me of a hanging case which we had here
three weeks ago, a young man was hung here by "Judge
Lynch" as they call it here, or "Lynch Law". He was a
gambler. One night he got into some difficulties with a miner
who was also gambling. This young gambler stabbed this
miner that he died next day. After the deed was done, the
young gambler went around to other gambling houses, and
boasted of it to his fellow gamblers. They told him that he
had better make himself scarce, as he might be hung. He
said was not afraid as he had plenty of friends in this place.
There were probably one thousand or more gamblers in this
town, so he thought they could save him in case that he*

would be taken up. But this was soon noised about among the miners, who soon arrested him, and held him under arrest till next day, when, in case the man who was stabbed died, he was to be hung.

Next day, about nine o'clock, the man died. And by this time there were already thousands of miners on the ground. They came in from every direction, hollering hang him, hang him, etc. The gambler, by this time, thought his chances to escape was rather poor because his friends could not do anything against so many miners. Therefore, as a last resort, he begged of the miners to let him send out for the sheriff, who was also one of his friends and who was out in the mountains somewhere on business. So the miners told him that they would give time till half past one o'clock PM. By this time, four or five gamblers were already on horses and started in going for the sheriff. They did not know exactly where he was so they went in different directions. In the meantime, there was great excitement going on. Some were for hanging him right away and some said let him see the sheriff.

Shortly after one o'clock, there was a great commotion in the crowd outside. It was announced that the sheriff was coming. He rode into the crowd as far as he could, then he jumped off from his horse and forced himself through the crowd into the ring where the prisoner was. His horse was all covered with foam and dirt.

When the sheriff made his appearance in the ring, the prisoner jumped up from the ground where he was seated and got the sheriff around his neck, so glad he was. The sheriff talked a little to the prisoner, then he came out into the crowd. There were several wagons standing close by. The sheriff got up on one of those wagons and the crowd was now silent to hear what the sheriff had to say. He made a little speech, and among other things, he said to the people they ought to have more respect for the community at large, and particularly the prisoner and that he would take charge of him and put him in "jail" and give him a civil trial. But he had hardly these words out of his mouth when they hollered again and said fetch on the rope. In a moment a rope came flying in over the crowd right upon the prisoners head. Meanwhile, the sheriff was still trying to be heard, but the crowd was now exasperated beyond control. So, they hollered again to fetch on another rope and take the sheriff too, and made a rush for him, but he went down over the wagon and through the crowd and was not to be seen any more.

If he did not leave as soon as he had, they would truly had taken him too, but he had just saved his bacon in time. They soon had the rope around the prisoners neck, and took him double quick down through town and out on a hillside where they soon had him strung on a limb of a tree.

On the way out of town the crowd was hollering, and cheering, like at a fox chase. After the man hung long enough to be dead, the crowd again dispersed and went to their respective quarters. Thus ended the hanging case.

I will now give you a few words in regards to my tramp to Sacramento City. Two weeks ago, I was agreeably surprised one day to see my old friend, and fellow companion across the plains, Mr. Kline, who came back from the city after a sojourn of about three months at that place. He was sickly nearly the whole time since he arrived in this country. He too had not taken proper care of himself after his arrival here, and like hundreds of others, contracted a decease called "diarrhea", of which a great many died. I too had a touch of it, but soon after got over it, as stated in my first letter.

Mr. Kline has not earned his board since he is in the country. And now he is going back to the states again. He is home sick, and says he cant stay here any longer. There is some of his friends going home, who will advance him some money to go with them. It will cost him about one hundred and seventy-five dollars from San Francisco to New York. He stopped with me two days, after which one morning we rolled up our blankets and started off. We miners always carrying our beds with us because lodging in bed cost one dollar per night and when we find our own beds and sleep on the floor, it cost only from twenty-five to fifty cents per night. I was told by some miners that they even pay one dollar for standing in a room per night. That was in the rainy season last year when rooms were so crowded that they could not even set down.

On the second day towards evening we arrived in the city which is situated on the east side of the Sacramento River about two hundred miles northeast of San Francisco. It is a place nearly as large as Lancaster PA. This is a pretty large place considering that it is not much more than a year old, however this has been a small town for many years. But, since the gold discoveries, it had increased almost beyond credibility.

From this valley, I can see the great snow mountains, which lay east from here, and distance about one hundred miles. They run north and south. On the following day Mr. Kline left me, for San Francisco from whence he will take a steamer for New York.

After staying two nights in the city, I left for the mine again in company with another man who came down with us, where two days afterward I arrived again in my old grants. I have as yet not had any big strikes. I am making from one to three dollars per day, but am a green horn at digging gold, and expect to do better after awhile when I get more in the way of it.

In my next, I will give you a description of the discovery of gold, how it was first found. Etc., and also a little of the gambling houses and gamblers and the doings on Sunday, etc.

I have laid in nearly all winter my supply of provisions which I need. All the miners who have money lay in a stock, in case the rainy season sets in. Provision will be much higher. All the stores are pretty well stocked with provisions.

I will now come to a close, hoping this may reach you all enjoying health, as it leaves me. My respects to you all. Don't neglect to write soon,

Yours respectfully,

D.B. Hackman

The hanging David witnessed during November or early December of 1850 was that of "Irish Dick" Crone. Following is an account recorded in the Gold Rush Chronicles[1]:

---

1 http://comspark.com/goldminer-mall/chronicles/hangtown.shtml

Crone Swings ~ *A lynching in 1850 resulted from an incident that happened at the El Dorado Hotel, when a miner accused a young monte dealer of "waxing the cards". The card dealer was Dick Crone (also called "New Orleans Dick", "Bloody Dick", and "Irish Dick", but not to be confused with "Rattlesnake Dick", an equally ornery character who terrorized Auburn for a time), who threatened to cut the miner's heart out if he accused him of cheating again. When the miner repeated the words, the gambler drew a large bowie knife, plunging it into the miner's chest twice, twisting it around the second time.*

Miners flocked into town from outlying diggin's to locate and punish Crone. He was found hiding in Coffee's Tavern, and was promptly tried (with witnesses testifying), convicted, and hanged that very evening by a jury of thousands.

The California Gold Country (Highway 49 Revisited) web site offers a brief vignette of the Crone hanging[2]:

This triple header was one of the earliest recorded lynchings in the Gold Country. It was followed by the hanging of "Irish Dick" Crone, strung up on the same tree for knifing a man to death over a game of cards. Several other bad men wore the hangman's noose and it wasn't long before Dry Diggings was known throughout the Gold Country as "Hangtown."

Further detail concerning the Crone hanging can be found at the History El Dorado California Chapter XXX web page[3]:

Such summary execution had the effect at least to intimidate the rogues, and put a restriction to the commitment of crimes for some time. This, however, did not last very long, for no sooner those outlaws observed that the watchfulness of the people gave way, and smaller crimes

---

2 http://malakoff.com/goldcountry/placervi.htm

3 http://www.westernlivingcenter.com/history/ch30-criminal_annals.htm

passed by unpunished, than they threw off their fear, raising up their heads and growing bolder than before. The result was another hanging of a desperado by the name of Richard Crone, going by the name of Irish Dick, a mere boy, after his looks, at Placerville in October, 1850.

He had crossed the plains from St. Louis in 1849, as a cook, but took to gambling as a profession and always was ready for shooting and fight. He used to keep a monte game in the El Dorado Saloon located at the site of the present Cary House, and one night a quarrel ensued there between two men.

Crone jumped up from his game and stabbing the one, he almost instantly killed him. After the act he deliberately wiped the blood from his knife and left the saloon; but after a long search was found hidden at Coffey's on Sacramento Street, where he was arrested. The murdered man had a brother mining at Chili Bar, and on account that those two hundred and more gamblers had always got the best of the miners, when the latter came to town, which was almost ruled by that class of men, the miners made up their minds that this business had to be stopped right there, and to the number of several hundreds came into town determined that Dick should die ; in which determination the better people in town concurred with them.

Dick was taken from the officers of the law and tried by two Justices of the Peace, one was Dud Humphrey, the other Wallace, in the presence of the excited thousands.

While here on trial, the spectators seemed to get impatient, but with the coldest blood Dick remarked to them: "Have patience, gentlemen: I will give you soon a fair lay out." The verdict was guilty; he was speedily taken by the crowd to a large oak tree, near where is now the Presbyterian parsonage, in spite of the officers, Bill Rogers, sheriff, and Alex Hunter and John Clark, constables, who fought desperately but powerless for the possession of the prisoner, the multitude being determined to see justice done and not to be trifled with, as often before.

The prisoner was placed under the tree with rope around his neck, he then begged for the privilege of climbing the tree to leap down from the fatal branch, but this was denied him, and he was jerked up by strong and willing hands.

A similar account is found among the stories of how Hangtown received its name recorded as "From the Notes of Frances Fairchild"[4]:

The sobriquet of Hangtown, by which Placerville was at one time only known, and which is now not infrequently applied to it, had its origin in the hanging by a mob in October of 1850 of a desperado named Richard Crone, but known to the community by the nom de plume of "Irish Dick". The fellow was but a boy, hardly more than 21 years of age, and came across the plains from St. Louis in one of the very first trains in the capacity of cook. He was of small stature and more noticeable because of his "outré" attire, a wide and peculiar mouth and large and protruding teeth. He took to gambling as a profession and showed by his skill and pluck that he was not unsuited for a business which especially at that time was a hazardous calling.

Like his fellows he never went unarmed, and like them would not hesitate to use his weapon when deemed it would aid his cause to do so. He soon made himself well known throughout the camps included in El Dorado County, but honored "Hangtown" most generally with his presence.

One night, while in the El Dorado Saloon where now stands the Cary House, he stabbed and almost instantly killed an emigrant who had just arrived, mistaking him it was said, for someone else whom he designed murdering for some fancied offense.

The murdered man had a brother in town who resolved that Irish Dick should die. In his determination the town concurred. Dick was taken from the place where the officers of the law had stationed him into the main street and tried by a jury of citizens in the presence of excited thousands, who had collected together from the surrounding country. The verdict was "guilty" and so soon as it was pronounced, the condemned was pushed from the temporary where on he and the sheriff and the extemporized court had sat, and

---

4 http://www.lfairchild.freeservers.com/custom.html

hurried along with the crowd toward the plaza, where preparations were made for his execution.

At this point the mob was told that a sick man was in the house nearby, and that the uproar seriously troubled him. The crowd, at once, returned down Main Street and up to what is now Coloma Street to a large oak, near where is now the Presbyterian parsonage. Meanwhile, Sheriff Bill Rodgers and Alex Hunter and John Clark, constables of the town, fought desperately for the possession of the prisoner, but against the determined multitude, they were powerless.

Throughout this terrible ordeal, "Dick", with his physical courage truly wonderful, conducted himself with the utmost coolness. When placed under the tree, with the rope around his neck, he begged the privilege of climbing upon the tree and leaping from the fatal branch. But this was denied him, and he was jerked up by strong willing hands, and was soon a dangling corpse.

Finally, the summary that appeared in the Mountain Democrat Jan. 11, 2002 (by Richard Hughey) sheds more light on the origin and fate of "Bloody Dick" Crone:

The winter of 1850 saw a dramatic increase in the population of sporting men, or gamblers, in Hangtown. They were immediately recognizable in their fancy dress clothes with the "biled" shirts. Haskins' "quiet and orderly town" was no more. "Fighting was a pastime, and shooting, upon the slightest provocation, was the chief amusement."

The miners lost large amounts of gold dust at the gambling tables, and in the endeavor to get even, continued to lose. The three-card monte sharpers of St. Louis were on the top round of glory, robbing the honest miners, who from curiosity put up their money to see how the thing was done. And they always found out.

Gamblers ranged from the infamous to the noble. A good example of the former was Irish Dick Crone. He had a troubled youth and learned his trade on river boat casinos. A diminutive man, he was insecure among his peers and over-compensated with pugnaciousness, and was prone to violence. He wasn't long in Hangtown before they were calling him "Bloody Dick Crone". The sobriquet was a

45

warrant of death in a mining camp. It was the second strike in a three strike town.

Predictably, the incident that ended Dick's career was a card game in the Eldorado Saloon on Main Street. A miner questioned Dick's dealing; the gambler took offense. In a flash the miner was on the floor, stabbed to death. The next day Dick was apprehended and brought back to the Eldorado for trial. A miners' jury convicted him of murder and sentenced him to hang.

The homicide might not have been judged a capital offense with another defendant, but Bloody Dick's reputation sealed his fate. The miners hauled him out to Elstner's hay yard and threw a rope over a stout lower branch.

Here accounts differ, naturally enough. It seems agreed that Dick offered to climb into the tree with the noose around his neck, and at a signal jump to his death. This was no stunt. It was a quicker and thus less painful way to die. According to Haskins and others, the request was refused as suggesting a barbarous act and setting a bad precedent. According to some writers, the request was granted and the crowd roared his approval when Dick came crashing down amidst the oak's leafy branches.

Chapter 10
Sundays at the Ureka Hotel

1851 in Hangtown, California, David writes his brother Andrew describing the local gambling houses.

Hangtown, California
March 9th, 1851

Dear Brother,

It affords me much pleasure to inform you that I have at least received some news from home. It is now better than a year since I have had any word from home. Your letter came to hand on the first of this month. And I am exceedingly happy to learn that you are all well and alive, with the exception of our dear grandmother, and Mrs. Frantz, who are no more. I am sorry for them and grandmother in particular. I was in hopes that we might both live to see each other once again. But time and tide is waiting for no one, and sooner or later we will all pop away, and be numbered among those that were here.

I noticed by your letter that you would like to be in California to dig gold. That is well said but there are many other things which you would perhaps not fancy so well. For instance, at home, you have a house and a good bed to sleep in, have anything to eat, and drink that you could wish for, go and see the girls, go to meeting with them, and besides enjoy all the comforts of this life, where as in this country you would be deprived of all the delicacies and pleasures of this life, and many hardships to contend with.

I would be very glad to have you here, but under the circumstances I would not advise you to come here. Should you however take the notion to come, do not depend upon making a big "pile" of gold, or you might perhaps be badly disappointed because there has not as yet been any very big strikes made. There is however plenty of gold here, but it

47

is scattered around so much that a person can't make more than from one to six dollars per day. I am now here nearly a year and have not had much more than a hundred dollars, clear of expenses, and work hard too, but sometimes I have to work a week or two and do not make more than my boarding. That is about the way it goes here in California.

I will also tell you of the beautiful weather that we have had all winter, there was hardly any rain this winter, and nice and warm almost like May, and June. The frogs and crickets were singing during January and February.

This fine weather has been the cause of nearly all these shanties that were built here in the fall, to be deserted. A great many miners left and went to other parts of the mines. I too, in company with another young man work about eight miles from here, up on the mountains but still occupy my shanty, as I come down every Sunday and sometimes Saturday afternoon, or evening.

How would you like to start off some evening and walk eight miles over the hills, down through deep gulches, across creeks and ravines, where there is nothing but a trail or foot path. Never no wagons can go through here, no hardly any horses, mules. You would not fancy it much I presume, and yet I do not mind it any more than you would walk eight miles on your nice level roads. Besides this, I carry all my provision from here up, twenty five, fifty, and sometimes seventy-five pounds, as this is our nearest place where we can get our provision.

Sunday is a great day in town. The streets are just literally crowded with people. Miners come in from every direction to lay their weeks supply of provision and some to gamble, and others to amuse themselves, and a great many spend, and risk their money on the gaming tables, all that they have made during the week. Saturdays and Sundays are great harvest days for the gamblers.

I will just give you an inside view of one of the gambling houses. There are three large ones and many smaller ones in this place. Now you will just imagine yourself to be down town, then turn around, and look up and upon your right, you will perceive a large building, upon the front of which is inscribed the name of the house, in large square gild letters "The Ureka Hotel". Finding yourself in front of its lofty doorway, you hear some very sweet music issuing therefrom. You will be desirous of knowing what is going on in the interior, a view of which cannot be had from the outside, on account of a larges screen being placed a few feet within the door. Entering therefore and passing behind the screen, you behold a spacious and oblong "hall", about sixty-five by eighty-five feet in size, the walls of which are richly furnished with magnificent mirrors and pictures of various shades and sizes. In the center of the room is suspended from the ceiling a large lamp sparkling with many brilliants, and on the sides and end, are many smaller lamps of similar finish.

On one side of the room is a spacious "bar", about forty feet in length amid a profusion of flowers, and images of beasts, parsons, and birds. Many decanters are standing, adorned with shining labels and filled with tempting wines and liquors of the best brands.

Behind the "bar" are four young men attired with special taste which attire consists of a red under shirt, and a fine white linen over it, no necktie and an open rolling collar, the short sleeves rolled up, above the elbows, no vest, coat or hat on, and around their waist, or hip, they wear a long red sash of very fine fabric, the ends of which are hanging down on each side of the individual, this besides boots, or shoes, and pantaloons the dress of the persons behind the "bar", besides a profusion of jewelry such as rings and breast pins, the latter is generally worn in its natural state. This dress is also generally worn by the gamblers, and many others. The sash however is universally worn by all the business community.

On the broad floor, are arranged at proper distances several large tables, besides many smaller ones which are covered with fine cloth, and on each table is a pile of gold and silver, coin, varying from one hundred dollars to five and ten thousand dollars. There are generally two persons to each table, one of them is shuffling and calling and distributing cards wile the other is receiving or paying out the money which is won, or lost, as the case may be. There are various kinds of games played on these tables, such as French Mountain Roulette, twenty-one, number and ABC games, and many others.

At one end of the room and elevated about midway from the floor and ceiling is the orchestra on stage with scenery up, which is a piano, and four other players, or different instruments, who are filling the spacious hall at short intervals with the best of music both vocal, and instrumental. These musicians are hired by the hour, at a certain sum, for the purpose of drawing large crowds, in which portion they are not disappointed, judging from the large and noisy crowd in the room. Here gambling and drinking is going on all night. A drink cost from twenty-five to fifty cents and cigars the same.

Leaving this house, and going up the street, you see nearly opposite from this another large house, with big letters in front, denoting the name of the house "The Eldorado". This is similar to the other one, only this employs a brass band.

In going still further up town on the right hand side there is another large house called the "Great Empire". These constitute the three large gambling houses, but there are many smaller ones, and always crowded especially on Saturdays and Sundays. These, in connection with all the other business going on naturally, creates quite a great stir, and commotion on such days.

I will here also give you a description of the mode by which the gold is separated from the dirt, or ground. The gold is all obtained by washing the dirt. We have a machine called the rocker, or cradle, so called because it stands on rockers, and in form resembles a common cradle, but instead of the headboard, it had a square box of about eighteen inches, by six inches deep, the bottom of which is sheet iron punched full of holes. The dirt which is to be washed, is carried into this box with buckets, the operator with a dipper in one had apply water, while the other hand he rocks the "cradle" not in a lullaby kind of fashion, but in short quick yanks, in order to keep the dirt moving back and forth in the box, till it dissolves, and runs through the perforated sheet iron beneath which is a slight wooden frame, in a slanting position, over which is stretched a piece of cloth. This is termed the apron, the dirt and water falling upon it. It is carried to the rear end of the cradle, in the bottom of which and about midway is places a cross piece *about three inches high which is called a riffle. Behind this, all the gold will lodge the dirt and gravel, being much lighter, and is therefore carried over the riffle and out at the tail end of the cradle. This washing is continued all day if desired, but when the days work is over, the gold, and dirt or sand, lodged behind the riffle is then scooped up into a large tin pan, after which it is finally separated by washing it out of the pan.*

The cradle must always be placed along side of a stream or pond. Sometimes we must carry the dirt a great ways, if there is no water convenient to where we get our dirt. There is generally only one or two to each machine. There is two of us working together. My partner has an interest in a log cabin up on the mountains, where we lodge during the week in company of four others. When we come to town we lodge in my cabin.

But, I must bring my letter to a close as the boys are waiting for me to go home with them. It is getting night and we have yet a good long tramp, and a lot of provision to carry. Direct your next letter to Hangtown, California, as we have now a post office here. Your letter cost me one dollar and sixty five cents by express, my love to all, and write soon.

Yours Truly,

D.B. Hackman

Chapter 11
In the Land of Gold and Doing Well

Hangtown, California
July 25th, 1851

Dear Brother,

I have anxiously been waiting for a letter from you for the last four months, but none has as yet come to hand. I am very anxious to know what you say about coming to California as you intimated in your last letter that you have some notion of coming to Cala.

But, I rather think that you have given up the notion to come out here especially as long as I cannot give you any very encouraging news from the gold regions. I am still in the land of the living and among the gold but the remunerations of my labors and hard living in California has not been very encouraging so far with the exception of the last four weeks.

We happened to strike a very good place where we make from six to twenty-seven dollars per day. There is eight of us in company. We have a machine called the "Long Tom". This is a kind of trough from six to eight foot long. At one end about two and a half feet wide and tapered off to about a foot wide at the upper end into which another trough is joined. At the end of this, another, and so on, for any desired length.

In order to work a "Long Tom", there must be a small stream of water to run through it. The dirt to be washed is thrown into the trough along the upper end of the trough. It must have a certain pitch or fall so that the water running through it will carry the dirt along with it to the lower or wide ones which is made like a scoop and the bottom of which is heavy sheet iron, punched full of holes. Here one man has a shovel or hoe and rakes the dirt back and forth till all the dirt is dissolved from the stone and gravel. The dirt and all that enters through the holes will fall into a box underneath in the middle of which there is a riffle behind which the gold will lodge.

Old tin type photo (circa 1850) of a Long Tom.

By this operation many hundreds of buckets of dirt can be washed in a day. But in order to get the water high enough up to give it fall we must sometimes build dams or bring it in ditches along the side hills or in spouts. We use at present, hose made of drilling which are about one hundred and twenty feet long.

We buy the drilling, cut it through the middle lengthwise and sew it together but they don't last very long. We wore one out in about four weeks. There was too heavy a pressure on. So we went to work and made one of strong duck canvas. We had a hard job to get all our fixtures here. In the first place we got our "Long Tom" and the connecting troughs at Hangtown. From there we had to carry them the eight miles up on the mountains where I stopped all winter. Here we worked with it during April and beginning of May when the water got to be low enough at the river.

We packed up and came over here about eight miles further but the first four miles we had it hauled for which we paid ten dollars. The balance of eight miles we had to *carry it again. On our way we had to cross a river so rocky that we could walk across on the rocks but it was also rocky to get to the river so much so that we had to lower our things down over a perpendicular rock onto those in the river with a rope, this being the only convenient place to cross with our burden except to go around a considerate distance. But we wanted to make our trip as short as possible and finally after many rests and much sweating we reached our destination. But we knew that it will pay if we get our "Tom" in running order once because we have been working several days with rockers.*

We are the only company so far up on this river because it is hard to get up here. We still go to Hangtown for our provision but I and another young man have a horse together so we ride or one of us at least. Coming back we pack our provision on his back.

One Sunday we were in town and in coming home I had the horse in charge. The boys took a near cut across the mountain while I had to go around. In coming up a steep mountain, within about a mile of camp and the horse following after me in a winding trail, he commenced to kick and jump and snort. I looked around but being several paces in front and dark too, I could not see directly what was the matter.

But among the things I had a sack with some potatoes on him which slipped around on the saddle and hung under his belly. Before I could catch him he started off down the mountain over rocks and through bushes that I thought he would surely break his neck, but he ran home to camp safe but my provision was scattered all along the path. Next morning I went back and picked up what I could find but my potatoes were scattered all over the mountain and could not find them all.

The river that we are working on is called the middle fork of Los Cosumne. We have already washed out over three thousand dollars for the last five weeks to be divided among eight of us. But four or five men could have done as much work in the same length of time. There is not enough work for all to work any advantage.

But perhaps in my next, I can give you more news about the diggings. I am better pleased with California now than at any time heretofore. I am getting more used both to the mines and to the mode of our life here. You can see by the description that our life in Cala is attended with a good many ups and downs but as long as I keep my health and have plenty to eat and drink I can get along.

Tell Mother, Brother Jacob, Uncle Isaac, and Aunt Fanny, that I am still in the land of gold and doing well. Write soon and direct your letter to Hangtown, California. Give me all the news from home and my love to all inquiring friends. Hoping this may reach you in good health.

Yours Truly,

D. B. Hackman

Chapter 12
Misfortune in the Best of Engagements

By late Winter 1852, David has moved to Mokelumne Hill, a town about 40 miles south of Hangtown (Placerville).

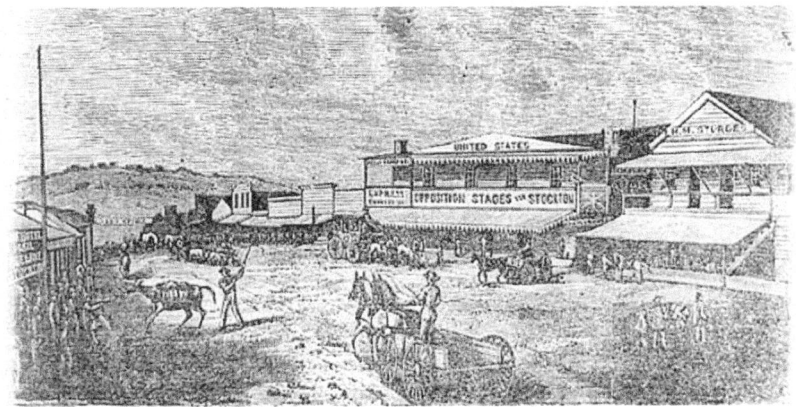

Mokelumne Hill circa 1854.

Mokelumne Hill, California
March 5ᵗʰ, 1852

Dear Brother,

I will again after waiting a whole year for an answer from you, take up my pen and address you with a few lines to inform you that I am still in the land of the struggling.

But I am almost discouraged to write anymore letters because I do not get any answers. It is now over a year since I got the first and also the last letter from you. Three days ago I walked eighteen miles to a post office where I ordered my letters to by express. When I got there I found none from you but there was one from Mr. Diffenederfer, Manheim, which letter cost me two dollars but I would rather have paid ten dollars than not to have it.

So you see we value letters from home very highly. This one and one from you are the only two letters that I received since I left home which is about two and a half years. I would be very happy to hear from you and also to get the news from home. I expect there has been many changes since I left home. I too have changed about considerable since last summer.

Last August after working out our claim on the Los Cumne River the company split up and some went one way and some another. We made about five hundred dollars apiece in a few months time. Four of us joined together and came south about seventy miles on a prospecting expedition.

We left everything back excepting our clothing, a few picks and shovels and cooking utensils. These we packed on our horse and the balance left on the claim for anyone to use it at their pleasure. In the course of about five days we arrived at a place about six miles east of Mokelumne Hill. Here were several deserted tents and shanties. We took up our quarters in one of these. Here I met with a great misfortune.

I had all my money stolen, excepting twenty-five or thirty dollars out of five hundred and some odd dollars. After stopping here for several days one of our partners the one who owned part of the horse, took the notion to go back to a place that we past on our way. He paid me the difference of the price of our horse and took him along.

I went along with him to Mokelumne Hill but my gold being rather unhandy to carry along, I hid it in a shanty while stopping on the hill. I met two of my old companions who came across the plains with me. They would not let me off so I stopped all night with them. Next day I went back again but as soon as I came in the shanty I saw that my gold was gone.

Being near dinner time and my two partners being out prospecting, I prepared dinner for us. They soon came back. I did not say anything until after dinner, then I told them that my money was stolen. They thought at first I was only jesting because I did not say anything sooner, but when I told them that it was really so, they took it much harder that I did. I thought it is for no use to make much fuss about it as it was gone and who got it I did not know. I am confident that none of my partners did take.

Here was one year of my labor gone to the shades. This has been rather a heavy stroke upon me, especially after working so hard as I did and besides having went through many hardships to obtain such a paltry sum and then lose it at the end. However, I had one consolation. There was plenty more to be had at the same price, which is by working for it. So I went to work in good earnest again but with very little success.

About this time there was a great excitement up on Mokelumne Hill, in regard to the deep diggings which they discovered there lately. My partners wanted to see the place so we went up one day and soon staked off three claims fifteen feet square to each man.

I did not want to go in because it was very expensive to sink deep holes and my purse would not hold out long. But they would not hear of a refusal and promised to see me through, let it cost what it may. Finally I consented. We took three more partners in with us and commenced to sink three shafts at different places.

We had taken our claims just in time. Next day every inch of ground was taken up all over the hill. We sunk three holes, one of sixty and one of ninety-two feet and the third we had down one hundred and thirty feet but could not work it any deeper on account of the water coming in.

So they asked us and two other companies adjoining them to go in with them and sink their shaft down and in case there is something in their shaft we could then sink ours down and if not there would be no use in us or the others adjoining them to go any further.

We all agreed to join them. So we divided off into our fours gangs and went to work for six days and nights we kept at it without any intermission. At the end of that time we came down on the bed rock or ledge, a depth of one hundred and fifty-two feet but no gold.

There were several hundred shafts sunk down but when we stopped our work more than half of the others deserted their claims and went off in every direction. One end of the hill paid richly but the end that we were on not one hole paid. We had to dig through a perfect wall of cement or "lava" as hard as flint. It cost us two dollars and fifty cents per day to keep our picks in repair.

There was seven weeks labor lost and all my surplus money gone and seventy-five dollars in debt to one of my partners who advanced me all the money I needed. This was the beginning of November but during the winter or rather winter season, as we have no winter here, I made enough to pay my debts and had one hundred and fifty dollars besides and a tolerable good prospect to make more.

Therefore I am still in good hopes and expect someday to have a small portion of the great wealth which is deposited in California. It is here, but it requires time and much labor to get it. There is money to be made here but the trouble is to keep it after we do make it. Misfortune however, will happen sometimes in the best of engagements.

A month or six weeks ago there was a great excitement in town one evening occasioned by the report that a man was shot by a woman in a small gambling house at the lower end of town which is occupied by Spaniards. There was soon a large crowd gathered in and around the house. The man was found to be shot on the spot. As soon as this was ascertained by the crowd outside they were calling to those inside to bring out the perpetrators of the deed but both the men and women of the house had vanished or *"Vamose"* the *"Ranche"* as the Spaniards say. The owner of the house not being forth coming, the crowd by this time becoming very large and excited they called out to demolish everything in the house and tear down the building.

Which was no quicker said than as many as could get at it, they commenced to demolish everything inside, wine and whiskey bottles, glasses, lamps, tables, and chairs, and everything that could be broken. When that was finished some procured ropes and tied them to the corners of the house it being only a one and a half-story frame.

They commenced to pull when they soon had it on the ground. They carried the whole thing on a vacant lot and set fire to it and in a very short time the whole thing was in ashes. On such occasions it is of no use for anyone to interfere because there is always some standing ready with revolvers and bowie knives to shoot or stab any one who would make resistance or interfere. Such is life in Cala.

We had a fine winter. No rain hardly and warm like last winter. I will now bring this letter to a close for the present hoping to hear from you soon. Direct your letter Hangtown, as I do not know where I may be by the time that you get this.

Love to all,

Yours truly.

D. B. Hackman

Chapter 13
The Trouble with "Grissilies"

Columbia, California in 1852.

By late 1852 David has moved to Columbia, 35 miles southeast of Mokelumne Hill in Tuolumne County.

Columbia, California
November 24th, 1852

Dear Brother,

After a lapse of eighteen months, I am once more favored with a letter from you. I came to the conclusion that you have all ceased to think about me, but I see by your letter that you still think about me.

I am exceedingly happy to learn that you are all well and anxious about me, especially Mother, but you can tell her that I am still in the land of the living and enjoy good health and if the Lord willing I hope that we may both live to see each other once again and also you and brother Jacob and our Aunt Fanny to whom I am deeply in debt for the service which she rendered unto me while I was sick at her and Grandmother's house.

I have been thinking about it many times since I am out here. I have written a letter to Uncle Isaac many months ago and have been looking for a letter from him before now but none has as yet come to hand.

Our mail facilities are so poorly arranged that many letters are lost, even after reaching California, and many packages are also lost on the "Isthmus" of Darien, as the transit there is made on pack mules and many mail bags are lost in the mud there as I was told so by one who came across the "Isthmus" this summer. This then may be the cause of my not hearing from you for so long.

I see by your letter that you still have a slight favor for Cala but have not made up your mind for certain yet.

You would perhaps like to have my advice in regard to the matter, but I cannot give you any better advice than what I have stated to you in a previous letter. Furthermore you will perceive by the progress which I make since I am here that the gold is not to be scooped up by the bushel but as I am here in this country I must do the best I can.

However, I am not the least discouraged so far, on the contrary the longer that I am here, the better I like it. We have such a beautiful and healthy climate here, and the winter seasons are so nice too. We have had very little rain and not even much frost, during the two winters that I am here.

My present location for the third winter is situated on "Experimental Gulch", one mile north of Columbia, There is only two of us in partnership, an old man who has been with me now nearly two years, and is also a Pennsylvania Dutchman like myself, as we are called out here.

We have a good log cabin to live in. Plenty of wood right on hand. It costs nothing but the labor to out it and carry it in. We have not yet laid our winter stock of provisions because provision at present is very high on account of the late great fires which we had in Sacramento City. The whole city was destroyed by fire and the greater part of Marysville, another large place situated about fifty miles north of Sacramento City, and thirty-two buildings in San Francisco. All this happened since October within a few days of each other. This caused the loss of many millions of dollars. This is one reason why provision is so high at present. Flour is thirty-two dollars per hundred weight; pickled pork is thirty-seven cents per pound; fresh pork fifty cents; beef twenty-five cents per pound; coffee thirty cents a pound; sugar twenty cents a pound; ham is forty cents; and everything else in proportion.

Sacramento Fire, 1852.

We have a good claim and also some honey and as long as we keep our health we have nothing to complain of. On the second day of this month we commenced to work our claim and washed seven days after waiting about three month for water. During the seven days we washed out two hundred and fifteen dollars. But then there is our expenses for water. Six dollars per day, which we get from the water company and twelve dollars for our boarding per week for both of us which is as cheap as we can board ourselves at present.

The reason why we did not work more days since we commenced is because the ditch broke twice since then and therefore detained us from work. If we would get plenty of rain this winter we could get enough water without paying for it.

In order to give you a better idea in regard to this water company or "ditch", I would state here that there is some organized companies who went to work and cut a "ditch" or "canal" around and over the mountains to some river to bring the water up to the gold mines. As the water in the river all lay hundreds of feet down in deep valleys between the mountains it is therefore necessary in order to get the water up front of these valleys, to go up into the mountains thirty and some even went as high as forty miles.

I worked about three months this summer for one of these companies at four dollars per day and board. There were some days two hundred hands at work. They had a boarding tent which they moved along as we advanced with our "ditch" over mountains and through valleys and across deep gulches. Here we had to build "flumes" in order to carry the water across these gulches from one mountain to the other.

In this manner they brought water down from the mountains a distance of thirty miles in a "ditch" three feet wide by two feet and a half deep. In the mines they branched it off in smaller ditches around through the mines. A small stream of water running through a box or spout for inch square cost eight dollars per day for the first head stream but after running through several machines it was cheaper when the water got to be thick and muddy, even as low as one dollar per day.

This may suffice to give you some idea about these ditches. We had considerable sport among ourselves up on the mountains while working on the ditch. We made noise enough some nights to frighten both the Indians and the grissily bears, both of which were plenty on these mountains.

But we dreaded the grissily bears more than the Indians. One Saturday afternoon several of us started off and walked to Columbia, about twenty-seven miles, merely to see the town. On the following afternoon or near evening we started to go back again but when we got pretty well up into the mountains we lost ourselves, there being only two of us. The others did not come back anymore.

After walking till about midnight, we stopped, built a big log fire and laid down to it. We both having six shooters, which we kept in readiness, in case of bears or other wild beasts making their appearance. But nothing molested us. Early on the following morning we started off and soon found our trail and about nine o'clock we reached camp.

On another occasion a young fellow we sent to town on a mule with some drills to get fixed. It got to be late by the time he had them fixed and being rather cowardly about wild beasts on these mountains, when he got within about four or five miles of camp, being late and very dark, his mule pricked up his long ears and began to snort and read up. The young fellow thought he was attacked by a score of grissily bears, so he jumped off of the mule and made his way on up a tree where he staid all night. This was the fellows own report but there was probably nothing but a mere trifle which frightened the mule. At any rate he came to camp after being left to pursue his own course.

Next morning before daylight, some four or five men started off in quest of the missing man. When they found him upon a tree the boys in camp run about it so much that he left camp the same day and went back to the settlements where there were no grissily bears. Such is life in the mountains.

Bull and bear fight in the Old West.

There were several bear traps around the mountains. Some bear hunters go to work and put up square houses built of logs firmly put together. At one end there is a door sliding up and down at the other end they fix a "bait" and in case the bear enters at the door and nibbles at the bait the door shuts down on him. After having one caged, they attach ropes around his neck and foreleg and hind leg and lead him to a town or city where they have a bull and bear fight with them. One or the other is generally killed and sometimes both.

I will now make a few more remarks in regard to myself. Having worked in the vicinity of Mokelumne Hill, as stated in my last letter, my old partner and I packed up and came down here where we are now quartered for the winter.

We left our tent and all of our tools and fixtures back and took only along what we could carry on our backs. The distance from there to here is sixty-five miles. After working around here awhile in the fore part of the summer but not making much on account of the scarcity of water, we bought our present claim and log cabin for seventy-five dollars of another party who wanted to leave this place for some other part of the country.

So you will perceive by this that we miners are ever restless moving about from one place to another. If we would be more contented and stay at one place we might do better at the end. A rolling stone gathers no moss as the old saying is so I will try and move about as little as can be helped as long as I stay in Cala.

I have no idea yet how soon I may come home. Not for a year or so at any rate. There is plenty of gold here but it requires time to get it. Once in awhile a person happens to hit upon a good place and takes out a large sum in a very short time. But as a general thing it is not so easily to be had even if we work hard. I will now bring this letter to a close hoping to hear from you again. Direct your letter to Columbia, Tolumna Co., Cala and send me some papers. I received one which was very interesting. Let me know if you received any papers from me. I sent several. Hoping this reaches you all in good health. Respects to you all,

Your brother,

D. B. Hackman

Chapter 14
The Old Dutchman's Dream

Yankee Hill is just east of Columbia, CA.

Yankee Hill, California
May 29ᵗʰ, 1853

Dear Brother,

I am once more again under may obligations to inform you that I received a letter from you which was dated April the tenth, and believe me dear brother, I am always glad to hear from home especially when the news are few and far between.

It affords me much pleasure to learn that you are all well and in the enjoyment of good health. I too am in excellent health, and have been since I left home. It is some time since I heard anything from you and all the news that I get is through you.

I wrote a letter to Uncle Isaac nearly two years ago, and several to Manheim, but no answers from either place, so I am dependent upon you for all the news. The last letter which I have written previous to this was in November last, but I sent you some papers in the interval. It appears that you do not get the papers which I sent to you. In that case it is hardly worthwhile to send them. Each paper cost me twenty-five cents. However two "bits" as we call it here is no object.

You say in your letter that you are glad that you did not come to Cala. I am pleased to hear you say so although I should have been glad to have you here. I think I told you enough in my previous letters to know that it is of no use for a person to come to this country with the expectation of making a big "pile" in a few months time. That is out of the question unless a person would have extraordinary good luck. As I said if a person would come here with the intention of spending a few years, he might probably during that time stand a tolerable good chance for making something because there are millions of dollars deposited in these hills and mountains throughout Cala which will never be taken out.

There is even now more gold taken out than what was taken out one or two years ago. Therefore it was thought that the gold mines would not hold out long because people only worked on the surface and in the gulches and ravines where it was more easy to be had. Now they are working into the banks and hills and even excavating mountains where they find richer deposits than in the gulch and ravine diggings.

Places where we had to dig down from two to five feet deep two years ago were considered deep diggings then but now we go down from eight to twenty and even several hundred feet deep and as a general thing miners do well.

I will now give you a few words in regard to myself. You will perceive by the heading of this letter that I have again changed my quarters, but this time I did not go very far— only about two miles from where I had my winter quarters.

Last March, my old partner and I dissolved partnership as our claim was worked out. He left me to go home or to Australia. He did not know which. We had close neighbors during the winter—old friends of mine—an old Dutchman, his son a young man about my age, and another young man with all of whom I got acquainted about two years ago and have been neighbors on several former occasions.

Their claim, also about this time, had given out, so we concluded to join together and go out prospecting. Consequently, one morning the old man's son and I started off one way while the other two went another course. In the evening we all came back and compared notes. They had not found anything which they thought would pay but in our tramp, during the day, we saw a claim which we could purchase for five hundred dollars.

After a short talk upon the matter we came to the conclusion to go and see it again the next day. Accordingly, on the following morning after breakfast, we all went together to make a further inspection of the claim.

There was a large pine tree standing right upon the claim, measuring about four and a half feet through or across the butt end. As soon as the old man saw the claim with the big tree on it, he said "this is our claim. I have been looking for one with a big tree or stump upon it for the last three years."

"There", said he, pointing towards the big tree, "underneath of that stump is the "big" lump of gold that I was dreaming of before I left home."

Of course he was only jesting when he said so. But upon the strength of his dream and the appearance of the claim we bought it before we went home. Next day we moved our quarters and engaged boarding at a boarding house close by, for the first time since I am in the country, at ten dollars per week and soon commenced operations.

But during March and April we had considerable rain. We are now about six weeks at work and took out about fourteen hundred dollars. Last Tuesday a week, we took out three hundred and seventy seven dollars. We are very much pleased with our claim and the nearer that we get to the tree, the better it pays. We are almost inclined to think that the truth of the old man's dream might be verified. There is strong evidence for it.

He often talked about his dream and said in Dutch, "Yah ich hab evva sella grassa stumba, noch net gafunna vu sell feala gold drunne stech un so long os ich sell net fin gana ich net is aim." (trans.: Yes, I have forever stumbled through the grass, not yet finding the great pile of gold I seek, but as long as I am able, it is my goal.)

This old man was seventy-three years of age. Three years ago, or early in the spring of 1850, he took the notion to go to California with two of his sons who were making preparations to go with a company starting from Zanesville, Ohio. But of late years, the old man was not very hardy and his folks told him that he was not strong enough to get through the many hardships that he would encounter on such a long trip and would therefore die before he would reach Cala.

He thought that he could stand it as well as his boys. Finally however, after much talking he consented to stay at home. But about two weeks before the company was to start he had his dream. He dreamed that he went to Cala and while there he saw a big stump and under that stump he found a big lump of gold.

When he got awake he woke his wife and said, *"Momma, now ganna ich noch Californy* (trans: Momma, I've decided to go to California)*", and she asked, "I worum donn don dandy* (trans: *Why* this big pronouncement?)*". He told her about the dream that he had and said that he was bound to go now, and go he did. Here he is now better than three years and never enjoyed better health in his life than he did since he left home.

The old man is in good hopes and says his dream will come to pass yet. We have certainly a good prospect and if our claim holds out any length of time at this rate, I may come home this fall or in the spring. I have some notion if I leave in the spring to go home across the plains. I think I would like it better than by water but I leave that subject for the present.

I have about five hundred dollars which I would like to send home as soon as I get an answer on this letter. I can send a draft on a Philadelphia bank which cost me four dollars per hundred. There is not much danger to lose it. One of my partners sent some home and as soon as I hear from that I may send mine also. But if I take a notion to go home this fall, I may not send it so. I may possibly keep it awhile yet. I have it on deposit in the express office at Columbia where it is safe for the present.

Express Office - Columbia, CA, built 1852.

I might mention here that we are again boarding ourselves. We only boarded out for four weeks. We would rather do our own cooking and have our bread, coffee, and pork and beans which we relish so much, as you do our beefsteak, chicken potpie or ham and eggs and I can sleep as well on my cot with an old coat for a pillow and a few blankets, as you do in your feather bed.

In this country a person gets used to almost any kind of life as long as we have our health. But, I do not know how I would fare if I should get a spell of sickness like you had in the fall. But sickness or death cannot be avoided lest us be at home or abroad. Of course home would be preferable by far.

I suppose you would all be glad if I would come home but I cannot yet comply with your wishes. I am now here nearly three years and yet the time seems very short to me. I expect it seems much longer to you, even though you have ladies to smile around you.

Women are not very plentiful here. There are some Spanish, Chileans and French and a few American women here but they are principally all fast, or women of bad repute. So, it is best not to have anything to do with them.

I omitted to mention above the high prices of provision during the month of February. We had nearly three weeks rain and the roads got so bad that no wagons could get through from Stockton, from which place all the provision to these parts of mines are hauled on wagons. There was very little stock on hand at this time and consequence was that everything was eaten up.

Flour sold for one hundred and seventy-five dollars per barrel; pickled pork seventy five cents per pound; beef fifty cents per pound; sugar & coffee the same. Some miners nearly starved. They could not cross the river. A great many miners left and went to Stockton and to Sacramento City. In those places provision was plenty, but they could not get them out into the mines. The first wagon that came into Columbia had a load of flour for some storekeeper, but before he got to the store, the miners jumped up on his wagon and took every sackful that he had. Of course they paid him for every sack, which was twenty-five dollars for a sack of fifty pounds. But, there were many teams on the

71

road and when they all came in provision were soon at old prices again.

I will now give you some more news in regard to our claim which is two days later than the above date.

Tuesday evening.

Today and yesterday we made some more big strikes. Yesterday it was raining but we worked about an hour and washed out one hundred and forty-eight dollars and today we washed about three quarters of a day and had three hundred and eighty dollars.

Now this is what we call a good claim. The best claim in fact is around Yankee Hill, but how long it will hold out we do not know. There is only a narrow strip that pays well—a kind of a lead which appears to run right under the big tree which is only about six feet off.

So, the old man is now, more than ever, under the impression that a big lump might after all be under that stump. But we will see when we get there. It will be some weeks yet before we get there. Probably in my next, I may be able to give you the result of the old gentleman's dream.

It seems however that fortune is smiling upon me of late. But I worked pretty hard since I am in this country with but poor success so I hope I might be favored with better luck hereafter.

I will now bring this letter to a close for the present, hoping to hear from you soon again. May this reach you all in the enjoyment of a good health, as it leaves me and the Lord grant that the day may not be so far distant when we might see each other once again.

If you would go to Manheim and see Mr. Diffenderfer, I left a portrait with him which I had painted while in Ohio. If he has it yet, please take it home. Direct your letter to Columbia. My respects to all,

Your brother,

D. B. Hackman

Chapter 15
Somewhat Deeper than a Manure Pile

Yankee Hill, California
July 3rd, 1853

Dear Brother,

I am once again the recipient of a letter from you which was dated May the sixth, and in perusing your letter I am inclined to think that you have again a small touch of the California fever as you would like to come out here, for the purpose of taking out the big lumps.

But you had better dispense of that notion, because the big lumps are not so easily to be raised out of their long depository places. They are deposited in the bowels of the Earth where no one can see them unless some one just happens to dig down upon them. These big lumps are not very plenty, yet there are many found at various sites, from one hundred to eighteen hundred dollars. But lucky are those who happen to find them.

And now dear brother if you have a serious notion of coming to California, for the purpose of trying your hand at gold mining you had better make up your mind and come at once and let the consequences be as they may. As you will with all probability come sooner or later but the sooner the better, unless you give up the notion altogether. This is about the best advice that I can give you. Of course you will take into consideration the many hardships and privations which you will encounter here and on your journey, besides being deprived of many comforts of this life which you are not aware of. However, nothing ventured, nothing won.

The next question is how far I live from San Francisco. The distance from here to San Francisco, is about one hundred and sixty-five miles by way of Stockton, and to Columbia and cost about fifteen or eighteen dollars from here there.

73

The distance from here to Sacramento City is about the same as San Francisco only that is further north from here. Our political laws are about the same here as they are in the States with some variations subject to new countries.

Farming is not as yet carried on to a very large extent, although there is some splendid farming land down in the valleys and along the "Coste". But up here in the mountains, there is hardly a level place containing more than from one to three or four acres which could be cultivated. But all these places are taken up around the vines here by parties who cultivate them and raise vegetables. I know a person last summer who had a garden of about an acre off of which he raised about two thousand dollars of vegetables.

In regard to the hills and mountains, your Furnace Hills or Allegheny Mountains are no comparison to our hills and mountains. So, you may imagine that I live in a different looking country than what you do.

I will give now a few more explanations in regard to my good claim, a few particulars of which I have already given you in my last letter. We have not taken out anything extra since my last, but I am still making from fifty to one hundred dollars per week. Still a tolerable good prospect to work all summer and probably next winter if it keeps on paying as it does now. At all events, I intend to stick to it as long as it pays if I live and keep my health. I have now upwards of nine hundred dollars after paying all expenses. My necessary expenses per week are nearly twenty dollars.

We have not yet worked up to the big tree, but in a few days more will bring us there. In order to give you some idea how we work our claim, I would state here that our claim is something like two hundred feet long and about the same width. We commenced at the lower end and worked it off in strips of about five feet wide—somewhat like you do when you haul manure only our pile or ground is somewhat deeper than a manure heap.

The further that we go into the bank, the deeper it gets. At the lower part it was two feet deep and where we are now, it is nearly twenty feet deep. About fifteen feet of this top ground has no gold in it so we have to throw that over where we worked it out and the balance of the dirt, from three to five feet deep, we wash. In these parts each man is allowed one hundred feet square for a claim.

I mentioned in my last letter about sending home some money, but I do not know whether best to send it or not. I would like very much if it was at home perhaps you could loan it our and draw a small percentage which would be better than to have it laying idle here. However, I will leave that for the present.

I will now with a few more remarks bring this letter to a close as I wish to take a walk down to Sonora, a considerable town about eight miles from here. Many of the boys are going down with me. Tomorrow we anticipate a glorious fourth of July. Both in Sonora and in Columbia, some of the large houses are going to serve up great dinners at four dollars a head and in the evening they are going to have a fancy ball which will cost ten dollars for admission.

Drawing of Sonora, California in 1852.

These places are principally patronized only by gamblers and other fast men and women of the place. On

75

these occasions there is always a great excitement and considerable fighting going on.

No more at present. I received no papers lately. I send you one every month. Hoping this may reach you in a more settled state of mind in regard to California.

My respects to you and all inquiring friends. Write soon, and direct your letter to Columbia, Tuolumne County, California.

From your absent brother,

D. B. Hackman

Chapter 16
"Helder Skelder"

Yankee Hill, California
July 27th, 1853

Dear Brother,

I am once more under many obligations to inform you that your letter of June 15th reached me two days ago. I am still in the enjoyment of good health and am happy to learn that you are all well and enjoying the comforts of this life.

I learn by your letter that my old friend, Mr. J. Diffenderfer, of whom I have in vain been looking for a letter, this long time, is no more. Well he has been with us for a short time but our Heavenly Father has seen fit to call him home out of the busy scenes and cares of this world. He has gone whence no traveler returns and after whom we all sooner or later must follow and be numbered among the past.

Further, I would state that I am happy to learn that you are still enjoying the pleasure and comforts of this life and cutting up around the ladies. I think if I was around the young ladies as long as you have been, I would get married. That is providing one of them would have me. There is always some exceptions to be made, especially where the ladies have something to say in it. But I have nothing more to say in regard to ladies because they are a great exception in this country. I did not even get as much as a kiss of a lady since I left the States.

I was in hopes heretofore that the day might not be far distant when I may have the pleasure of seeing you all again but another unfortunate circumstance occurred which will with all probability detain me another six months or a year in this country. I may perhaps be able to give you a better explanation upon this subject in a short time. I still

*am at work and making a little money but we have not been
making anything extra for the last three or four weeks.*

*Last week we excavated the big tree until he fell over.
We were digging around it and cutting off the roots. We
brought our stream of water to wash away around the roots
which are nearly three quarters of a days work. We had the
pleasure seeing him toppling over.*

*But we were all more or less disappointed because the
"Old Man's Big Lump" was not forthcoming. Soon after
working past the tree and finding no extra pay. The old man
talked about selling out and go home. He said, "ich dank ich
now my grosse glumbs, now will ich hein nach house ga,
szu der Momma."* (trans.: I think I am now very sad. Now I
will head for home to see the wife.)

*So he will probably sell out the first opportunity that he
gets and go home. I should indeed be sorry to lose him as a
partner because we have been much together for nearly
three years now and has always been a good friend to me.
So I am ready, I would go with him, whenever he goes, but
that will hardly be so now.*

*You speak about making hay. I think if you had your
grass here, you might cut it in the evening and haul it home
in the morning because there is not a particle of dew falling
during the night and would not need to be in apprehension
of getting rain upon it because there is no rain here all
summer. You cannot even see a cloud for weeks and months
at a time. We have very hot days but cool nights and after
all we have the most healthy country that a person might
wish himself unto. I do not say that because I am enjoying
good health myself but I am here among hundreds of people
almost and yet I must say that I have not seen a person
who had died a natural death for two years although there
are some dying here as well as in other countries.*

*But as a general thing they are very few considering the
many thousands who are sojourning in this country. There
is more persons killed both willfully and accidentally than
there was dying a natural death. Some get shot and
stabbed in rows and quarrels and some are hung and many
are killed accidentally throughout the mines in excavations
etc. Many get killed as above stated, and yet it is a great
wonder that not more are killed in this country because*

there are so many different people here almost from every nation and clime on the globe.

Here we have the Americans, Dutch, Irish, Spanish, Mexicans, Chileans, Italians, French, Chines, Japanese, and a few Polanders and many native California Indians and others. All more or less in contact with each other, each one having a different language, none of which I can understand except Dutch, Irish, English and a little Spanish which is the easiest language to learn of any foreign languages.

You would laugh if you could see about a dozen or so of Frenchmen together and hear them talk. If one of them begins to talk upon a subject they all commence to talk upon the same subject. I can't compare it to anything better than a lot of geese when they are frightened and commence to jabber and make a noise together. Each nation generally keep their own public houses where there is many of their people at one place. The French generally keep "restaurants", the Chinese boarding houses. I generally take meals at their houses when I go to town. They keep the best "table" of any. The Spaniards and Mexicans go in for dancing houses or "Fandangos", as they are called, but these are tolerable rough places. These places are very often stormed or demolished by gamblers and rowdies of the town.

Several weeks ago, a half dozen or so of these rowdies one night entered one of these houses with pistols and bowie knifes in hand and run everybody out of the house. Some of the men and women jumped out through the windows helder skelder. After the house was clear, they commenced to demolish everything that was in the house. Next day they came around and asked for their bill of damages which was to the amount of about four hundred & fifty dollars, which they paid and went their way.

This is nothing very uncommon here. They do anything when they get on a bender or three sheets in the wind. I need not give you any description of gambling houses, because they are the same here as elsewhere and very often shooting and fighting at these places.

A few nights ago, I was looking in one of the gambling places, when one of the gamblers and another man got to quarreling. Then one of them drew his knife while the other one drew his six shooter and fired at the other across the table. But in the excitement, he missed him and the ball flying over the heads of a crowded room and passing through a lamp at the other end of the room. Soon a dozen or more of pistols and knifes were waving overhead and gleaming in the light, ready to pitch in at short notice if there was any fighting to be done. But everything passed off without anybody being hurt. Such is life in California.

I will now come to a close for the present, hoping to hear from you soon. If you see old Christian Hershey give him my respects and tell him I am well and hope to see him before very long.

Also tell mother that I am still in the land of gold and enjoying good health. My respects to you and brother Jacob and family and to all inquiring friends, and to your ladies in particular.

You mention in your letters that you do not get any newspapers. I send you one almost every month but it appears that you don't get them. I received but two from you yet.

No more. Direct your letter as before,

Yours respectfully,

D. B. Hackman

Chapter 17
Iron Spoons, Pork and Beans

Yankee Hill, California
October 7th, 1853

Dear Brother,

I am again happy to inform you that your letter of August 17th reached me a few days ago and I am much pleased to learn that you are all enjoying good health. I can say as much of myself, in fact I never enjoyed better health than I do since I am in this country.

Since my last letter things have changed about considerably. The old gentleman and one of the other partners sold out to another party of two and went home. After working a week or so after they sold out.

The old man's son and I transferred our shares to another party and left the old claim. I received one hundred dollars for my share. Some of the others got as much as two hundred dollars. The reason that I got the least for my share was on account of having sold out last and the claim paying less every day would hardly pay expenses anymore and water rent was six dollars for every day that we washed.

There was at this time another claim for sale about half a mile off which I thought would pay if worked right and also plenty of water during the winter without paying for it which was considerable of an item. Therefore the old man's son, (who was still with me) and I, and two other men went and bought this claim for one thousand dollars, or two hundred and fifty dollars apiece.

We have been at work at it now about six weeks, but have consumed nearly all this time in clearing off and making ready to wash as soon as we get plenty of water. We have not water sufficient at present to work much. But we are very well pleased with our bargain so far. Week before last we ordered some lumber from a saw mill about two miles from here with which we built ourselves a nice frame shanty. Put up some nice bunks to sleep upon. They are fixed at one end of the room, two above and two below. The first two are about two feet from the ground and the others three feet above the others and in place of a bed cover we have canvas nailed across. Then in order to have it a little more comfortable, I made myself a chaff back, but instead of chaff, I put some leaves in it.

Then we have also a window of two panes of glass in our shanty which is quite a commodity as we need not look through the cracks to see daylight. Then we have also boards nailed upon stakes driven into the ground for a table which is also more convenience than to set down upon the ground to eat. One gable end is altogether taken up with the chimney and the door. I have done masonry work at the chimney while the boys carried the stones to hand.

We have done nearly all our work at the "shanty", during the hours of rest at noon and in the evening after being through with our days work in the mines. My Saturday evening we had it all finished to our satisfaction, and on the last Sunday we had a regular flitting, upon which occasion we also had an old fashioned "Pot-Pie", minus chickens, but instead we had beef. I have been detailed as the chief cook, being considered the most proficient hand at the culinary art. I was very much complimented both by my partners and a gentleman, an old acquaintance of ours, who we invited to our dinner and who said that he had nothing to equal my "Pot Pie" since he left home. We also had few bottles of the ardent "spirits" to enliven us a little on this occasion.

We had an old "log cabin" on our claim, but it stands down in the gulch, and in time of rainy weather the old concern is always inundated by the least little flow, in consequence of which we left it and about as above stated.

I will further make a few general remarks in regard to our mode of living as it may probably be interesting to you. As I stated above, that I am chief cook, I have theretofore all the time allotted to me which I require for that purpose while the "boys" keep at work on the claim during that time.

But I don't require much time for my culinary affairs as we have principally but one "dish", which consists of a pot full of "pork and beans". The beans are hulled. After supper I generally put my beans in the pot or kettle and leave them boil awhile, after which I put in a tolerable good slice of pickled pork, a little pepper and more salt if required. Then keep a good fire until I retire for the night. Leave them hang over the file all night, in the morning while the coffee is boiling, the pork and beans will be ready to serve which is set upon the table, pot and all. Each one having his own tin cup for coffee, tin plate, knife, fork and iron spoons. Each one helping himself to as much as he needs. Bread we generally buy in town to last all week but in case of not holding out I bake a small loaf and sometimes I have pan cakes or Slap Jacks, as we call them here. After being through with our meal, each one turns his plate upside down to keep the flies off from it, where it is left till wanted again. The pot of beans, I take, and a little water and another small slice of pork, which I set over a slow fire and leave it till noon when after making coffee. We go through the same process.

But after dinner if I think that my pot won't hold out for supper, I add a little more water, a few sliced potatoes and little more pork which is again set over a slow fire till supper time. As we work close by, I run in sometimes and inspect the fire but sometimes I forget myself and have my whole pot of pork and beans burned to a crisp. But accidents will happen in the best of families, so ours is no exception.

So you will perceive that we have pork and beans all the time. But one of the "boys" says that we must have a change sometimes and have pork and beans for breakfast and beans and pork for dinner, and pork, beans and potatoes for supper. He says he gets tired of it if we do not change it. He is the only one among us who has a china plate to eat off of but he says he won't wash it more than once a week because he is afraid that it will wear out too soon. So we wash our dishes only once a week, generally on Sundays when we also do our other washing and mending of cloths. I believe this is about all that I can give you in regards to our life in California.

I am better pleased with my present home than I have been at anytime heretofore since I am in the country. We have laid in nearly all our winter and stock of provision.

Thus you will perceive that I am again settled for the present and do not expect to come home before next summer at least.

I omitted to mention that the old man's son sold out again shortly after we bought in here for what he paid and went to Columbia into some other business. So I have all strangers for my partners but I am well pleased with them so far.

You mention in your letter that Mother made inquiries in regard to me. Well fine, and if you please inform her that she need not be uneasy about me and that I will not forget what she requested you to tell me and tell her to accept my heartfelt thanks and gratitude for her kind remembrance of me.

Enclosed you will find a lithographic view of Columbia our nearest town, which is a true representation of the town and surrounding country. The rainy season has not yet set in for which we are waiting in order to get a sufficient supply of water to go on with our work.

We have beautiful weather yet. Hoping this may reach you all enjoying good health and write soon. Direct your letter as usual. My love to you all,

Yours truly,

D. B. Hackman

Chapter 18
Tears Rolling Down Over Grim Visages

Christmas 1853, David marks his letter from Columbia. It is not clear if he is still prospecting at nearby Yankee Hill.

Columbia, Tuolumne County, California
December 25ʰ, 1853

Dear Brother,

I will embrace the present opportunity to inform you that I am still in the enjoyment of my usual good health, hoping this may reach you all enjoying the same.

I have not heard from you for the last four and a half months. I received the Lancaster Examiner & Herald, which contained very interesting news to me. Anything from or near home, is interesting to us who hear or see so little of home.

My old friend and former partner sent a letter to his son stating that he reached home in thirty-four days after leaving us and that he is perfectly satisfied with his trip to California but he said if he was a little younger yet he would come out again but as it is now he will never see California anymore.

The times here are brightening up a little more from what they have been for the last two months. A great many miners have been idle on account of the scarcity of water. This has been an unusual dry season. The rivers got so low that the water companies could not furnish half a supply of water for the mines. But according to present appearances there will be plenty of water soon if it keeps raining awhile yet.

But I cannot give you any favorable account. I am still digging away for gold with but slow progress. I have nevertheless a favorable prospect ahead which may yield me enough during the winter and spring to enable me to come home by next summer if I live and keep my health.

I have a desire to see home and friends once more even though I do not expect to remain at home. I am not sick nor tired of Cala but misfortunes seem to follow me wherever I go. I am now better than three years in this country and yet I am not much better off than what I was when I first arrived here in this country.

I mentioned to you in a previous letter of a circumstance which I said would probably detain me in this country for some time longer than I had intended to stay. And so you would wish to know what I have done with the nine hundred dollars which I mentioned to you in a former letter that I had ready to send home.

I would merely state here that I loaned out six hundred & fifty dollars at three percent per month (the rate of per cent here is from three to five and even as high as ten percent per month), and two hundred and fifty dollars I paid into this claim which left me only a small balance on hand.

I loaned the money out in July, for three months. I got for security three yoke of oxen and a trug wagon which would have covered more than the amount but the wagon and one yoke of oxen was taken from my by three who claimed a better right than I had. Therefore, I am not able at present to tell you how I will make out. I will however give you a further explanation upon the subject hereafter.

I have yet three hundred dollars, for which I will enclose a draft for that amount which will probably reach you by the first or second week of February. If I had sent my money home as fast as I made it I might be worth considerable more than I am now. But if we knew everything before hand we would soon be rich or perhaps quite crazy, which would be equally lamentable.

The draft which I sent to you will be payable in a bank in Philadelphia, but you can get it cashed in Lancaster by most any of the merchants there who have dealings in Phila.

Last Sunday I went to Columbia and as the mail had just arrived there was a great rush for the office long before the mail was changed. All were anxious to get news from their distant homes. But many are disappointed. There is always a great "rush" when the mail comes in but especially so when the mail comes in on Sundays because there are hundreds and even thousands of persons who come in from every direction of the mines.

Post offices throughout the mines are few and far between, and miners will go five, ten, and even twenty miles for letters. They elbow their way along with the crowd to the delivery box with eager and fond expectations of receiving some news either from parents, brothers, sisters, friends or sweethearts as the case may be. And when told by the postmaster that there is nothing for them they turn away in sorrow and disappointment and some cases tears rolling down over their grim visages.

While those who were more fortunate and received letters, turned to one side out of the crowd, with their much coveted letter or billet, which no money, in many cases, could buy, unopened, and tearing off the outer cover read it with avidity. That might truly be envied by those who went away empty-handed.

There is no such thing as rushing up to the letter box because each one must fall into line, not of "Battle", but of impatience, because the hindmost ones have to wait sometimes a long time before they get up to the box as there is very often five hundred and more in one line.

No one can ask for more than one letter except of the same name. I have seen persons pay as much as one dollar to buy men out of the line who were in front and take their place. If anyone would be foolhardy enough to force his way into the office or slip into the line in front regardless of the rules and regulations, he would soon have half an ounce of cold "lead", or a few inches of "steel" run through him.

This inadequate description may perhaps enable you to form some idea how highly we Californians value letters or any news from home. Perhaps in my next letter I may be able to give you better news in regard to my claim as we have not yet had sufficient supply of water to get a fair trial. So, I will abide my time and live in hopes the weather here does not correspond with your Christmas weather. In place of cold and snow, we have nice and warm, such as you may expect to have during the months of May and June.

And turkeys, geese, and chicken, we have none either. But in place of that we received a present from our store keeper on the hill here, which consists of one bottle of brandy, one box of sardines, one can of oysters, and one can of lobster, all of which was appreciated very highly by us.

I will now with a few more remarks bring this letter to a close, hoping to hear from you soon. Please give me the address of our Uncle Hackman in Indiana and other relatives living in the west.

As one of my partners contemplates going home next spring or summer, he lives in St. Louis, Missouri and I may probably accompany him home and call on some of our friends on my way.

If you see Uncle Isaac, give him and family my respects and tell him that I am still looking for an answer on the letter which I wrote to him a year or so ago.

Give my love to our dear mother and tell her that I expect to see her before very long if I live and keep my health.

No more at present. Direct your letter as usual and accept my respects,

Yours truly,

D. B. Hackman

Chapter 19
A Few Incidents in Regard to the Indians

Columbia, California
February 20ʰ, 1854

Dear Brother,

I have at last after many disappointments the pleasure of informing you that I received your letter on the nineteenth, Ints, which was dated January 17ᵗʰ. You have kept me waiting for a long time. The last letter which I received, previous to this one was dated August 10ᵗʰ, so you will perceive that is nearly or quite five months that you have kept me in anxious anticipation and disappointment for a letter.

But no matter now, since I learn through your letter that you are all well and enjoying good health. I am glad that I received this letter because I enclosed a draft in my last for three hundred dollars, knowing thereby that you will be at home to receive it when it comes. I have most anxiously been looking for a letter for the last three month. I knew that there ought to be a letter for me but at every inquiry at the office I was disappointed until last Sunday evening I had the pleasure of receiving one. So there is not much lost, only a few eager anticipations, that is all.

I would further state that I am still in the gold fields and enjoying my usual good health. Hoping these lines reach you in a better state of health than what you have enjoyed for the last few months prior to your letter. Speaking of sickness, as I learn in your letter, that was prevailing in your neighborhood during the fall, reminds me of our pleasant and healthy state of this country. I think I would not exaggerate the truth, if I would assert to you that I have not seen more than two or three cases of sickness for the last year, and deaths I have not seen for the last two years, and yet I am in contact with hundreds of people weekly of different classes and stations. So you may imagine that this is a healthy country. As a general rule, people in the Pacific states all look well and more hardy than in the Atlantic states, with but few exceptions.

As I stated above, I am still in the gold fields but not making money quite so fast as I should like to make it. But since the various misfortunes that have overtaken me, I do not expect to obtain a very big "pile" for the time that I intend to remain in this country unless I should make it now in a very short time.

I have made up my mind to leave the country sometime during this spring or summer. However, I will not specify any particular time as it depends altogether upon circumstances. So you need not expect me just yet.

In regard to that draft, which I sent to you. If you receive it you may loan the money out as you think proper but not as I did mine here, that you can't get it anymore when you want it again. I may perhaps send you another draft soon. I have not so much together now as I would like to have. I always like to keep enough on hand to go home on. If you get these three hundred dollars, I wish you would let me know how much money you have of mine altogether as I do not know the amount exactly. After waiting a long time, I have finally received a letter from Uncle Isaac. He had written several but by moving about from one place to another it appears they have not reached me. I am happy to learn that him and his family are all well. I have sent him an answer two weeks ago, in which I have given him about all the particular news which transpired here.

In regard to newspapers, my partners and I get all the financial news twice a month, which are sent out here from a few of the principle cities at the east, namely New York, New Orleans, Boston, and St. Louis and others. These are about all the papers which are sent out here and carried around through the mines at twenty-five cents apiece. We got about all the principle news through these papers that transpires in the States, but the news of these papers are not so interesting to me as those from our native homes.

Having nothing of importance to write at present, I will give you a few incidents in regard to the Indians, of their habits, dress, and mode of living.

90

There are a great many Indians here of various tribes, but no tribe contains a very great number, because they are divided into almost numberless tribes. They are generally of small stature, and very lazy, dirty, and filthy. They have a peculiar way of disposing of their dead and may be seen by the following.

Last summer there was a tribe encamped only about a half a mile from us. One day it was reported that two young married Indians died accidentally. However a number of them had been to town, and they are very fond of whiskey or "firewater" as they call it, and two of them belated themselves and on their way to camp in the night, they both fell into a ditch or hole, and were both dead when found. On the following evening after, it was noised about that they found two of their men dead and were going to dispose of them that night.

So a parcel of us "boys" went over to see the performance. When we arrived at their camp we noticed a large pile of wood and brush which about nine o'clock they set fire to. After which they brought forth their dead and piled them on top of the wood which was now burning freely.

Two or three were now tending to the fire, piling on more wood, while all the others formed a circle around the fire, both male and female, old and young. At a given notice from one of their number, they all commenced to run and dance around the fire, whooping, yelling, and humming in a death requiem and cutting up various performances.

The wives of the dead men were in care of one or two "squaws" outside of the circle, also yelling, moaning, and dancing, and once or twice they ran into the circle and wanted to jump into the fire which they were prevented from doing by some of the Indians taking hold of them and dragging them outside the circle again. They continued their death frolic until the dead bodies were all burned up.

The Indians here in this part of the country generally have not much clothing. Some of the men have pants on while others have only skins, or other material tied around their waist or hips and a blanket or a skin thrown over their shoulders. The "squaws" generally have a kind of a petticoat on and a blanket or something over the shoulders, nothing on their heads or feet. They often come to our shanty for something to eat, or some clothing. The other week we had a cold drizzly rain, when a young Indian came to our shanty. He had nothing but a blanket on his shoulders. He asked us, by motions, (of course), for a hat and shoes. One of my partners gave him a pair of boots and an old straw hat. We showed him how to put on the boots. He sat down on the ground and tried to put them on but it was a no go.

So I made him set down on a stool. I stood astraddle of his leg and after twisting and pulling a long time, I got them on for him, which were rather pinching his toes. After putting on the hat which was also about two sizes too small, he strode up and down the shanty a few times in high glee, after which he left.

A few days afterward we met him again among a number of other Indians, minus a hat, or boots. We ask him where he had the boots. He shaked his head, and pointed to his feet. They were too tight and his feet were all blistered up. He pointed to another young Indian who had them on.

These Indians principally live on wild game, acorns and grasshoppers. They have a novel mode of catching grasshoppers, which are plenty in the fall season and considerable larger than those in the Atlantic states. The Indians go to work and dig out innumerable little holes in the ground, wide in the bottom and narrow at the top. After this is finished they form a large circle and chase the grasshoppers together in the holes out of which they cannot very easily get when in once. After they have all in they want, they scatter dry grass and leaves over the holes which they set fire to. This will scorch the grasshoppers and burn their wings and legs off. After which they pick them up and eat them.

This is one mode of catching them. They sometimes go out where there is many grasshoppers and set the grass on fire, which is dry. Afterward they go and pick them up. The Indians do not eat salt meat of any kind, but they go in for something sweet. At one time there were three or four squaws came to our shanty. We were just eating supper. They were talking and pointing to each other about the different things we had. After being through, we offered each a tin cup full of coffee and some bread and salt pork but they did not relish the pork.

Seeing a bowl with sugar on the table, one of them poked her finger into the coffee and stirred it around and pointed to the sugar, intimating that they want sugar in their coffee. So we gave them some. This pleased them very much. After being through with their bread and coffee, they left us.

I will now give you a few more particulars in regard to our claim which is two days later than the above. Yesterday being Monday, we made seven dollars, which was one dollar and six bits to the hand. That was about as much as we expected. But today we expected about eight dollars to the hand, but to our inexpressible delight we made seven times that amount. We were not long at work this morning when one of the "boys" picked up a lump of gold worth fifty-seven dollars and shortly afterward another one of the "boys" hollowed out and picked up another lump of one hundred and thirty dollars and forty dollars in fine gold which made the sum total for today two hundred and twenty-seven dollars.

So you will perceive by this, that we do not know what is before us. One day we make nothing and the next day we might take out enough to pay us for many days lost time.

After today's good work, we are not certain that we can make our "grub", tomorrow. But I must come to a close and take this letter to town as the mail will close in the morning.

Give my love to Mother and her family and tell them that I intend soon to come home, if I live and keep my health.

Write soon and tell me how you are all getting along. You may look for some papers. Give my respects to all inquiring friends and accept a portion for yourself. Direct your letter as usual,

Yours respectfully,

D. B. Hackman

Chapter 20
"Tom", "Dick", or "Harry"

Columbia, California
March 25ᵗʰ, 1854

Dear Brother,

Your letter with the receipt of that draft duly reached me on the 22 Inst., for which I am very thankful as I have at least that much saved. The contents of your letter contain many truths, especially in regard to sending my money home.

I see the mistake but too well, however it is too late to recall the past. But the facilities for sending money home were generally not so good heretofore as they are now. It is true, if I had sent my money home as fast as I made it, I might be worth considerable more than I am now, but there is where I made the mistake. So I will try and do better in the future.

You inform me of the large hogs that you slaughtered this winter. A few yards of sausage and a few pounds of pork would be quite acceptable as that is something that we do not get here. I will make a few remarks in regard to your corn speculation, as you say. If you had known two weeks previous what you knew two weeks later, you might have realized a small fortune, but you did not know it. Consequently you did not run the risk. So we will take that in comparison with my bad luck and I think it will come out even.

You also state in your letter that there is several gentlemen here in Cala from Lancaster County. I have never come across the first person whom I knew in Pennsylvania or any other state since I am in this country. To look up a person here would be like hunting for a needle in a stack of hay, unless a person chanced to pop right upon him.

Persons here seldom know each other by name. We often see persons every day, converse with them, and be among them for weeks and months at a time, and yet do not know their proper names. This is a very common occurrence here. Most every person has a nickname. We generally answer to any name by which we are addressed, which is commonly "Tom", "Dick" or "Harry", or "Cap", "Major", or "Colonel", or some other nickname.

The next part of your letter informs me of your wish to be in Cala for six months only. I am rather inclined to think that you would get enough of Cala ere the six months were up, because we could not very well afford to board you on ham & eggs, chicken potpie, roast turkey, etc. But we could give you some beef and for a bed we would give you a good soft clapboard to sleep upon. Therefore I am inclined to think that you would not fancy our mode of living very much. In fact, six month would hardly be long enough a time to get initiated to our mountain life. As for the gold, you could obtain in that short space of time, would hardly pay you for your hard living and Cala life as we call it.

And besides this, you would also be deprived of the agreeable company of those ladies, which you stated in your letter, who are coming to see you occasionally. You must be in luck if you have them coming to your house. Some of these days, when I would like to have the choice of one or two at least. But I have nothing more to say in regard to ladies, as I have nothing to do with them here, because they are rather an expensive commodity in this part of the country.

I will now give you a few words in regard to myself. In the first place, you would like to know how much money that I have got. That is easy told. I have just got the sum of two hundred and twenty dollars laid by, to take me home when I am ready.

I expect to realize about five or six hundred dollars out of the claim yet. That is what we hold each share worth at present. I may not get that much and on the other hand I might get a great deal more. There is no telling how much money there is in our claim. We have not taken out any big lumps since my last letter but we have had some good days since.

In the next place, I will give you a few words in regard to those six hundred dollars which I loaned out last summer. All that I have got towards that is two yoke of oxen for which I may get two hundred and fifty or three hundred dollars. I have then on a "rancho" in pasture, down in the valley about thirty miles from here. I intend to bring them up in the mines next week and sell them for what I can get for them. The balance, I presume, I have to wait till I get it. Thus the matter stands with me at present.

I have nothing more to say, except that I think I will hold on a few months longer before going home as I am not quite so anxious to leave now as I was some time ago. But I still would be glad if I was ready to go home.

No more at present hoping this may reach you all enjoying good health, as it leaves me.

Give my love to all inquiring friends and to your ladies in particular, and reserve a portion for yourself. Write soon and direct as usual.

Yours truly,
D. B. Hackman

Chapter 21
Shock the Modesty of Any Lady

In 1854 at Columbia, David is alone but reflecting upon his life as a prospector. He wrote his brother Andrew concerning the activities in the town and nearby mines.

Saturday Evening
April 7th, 1854

Dear Brother,

I have just returned form our mountain village, which is situated one and a half miles from our camp. We generally stop work on Saturday noon or early in the afternoon and go to town in order to exchange our gold dust for coin and see if there is any news from home; also to see the fashions as we call them, some of which would be enough to shock the modesty of any lady, especially those fashions which are worn by the Indians.

They generally put on any piece of clothing that they can get a hold of. Saturdays and Sundays there are generally many Indians as well as other folks coming to town. At one time, there were a lot of Indians in town on Sunday. One of them had a high silk hat on his head and a long blue and yellow tail with buttons and a shirt—which was all that he had on his person.

Another one had nothing but a shirt on and others only pants, but the one with the silk hat took the shine off of all the rest and felt about as proud as we generally do with our best Sunday go-to-meeting duds. Many of the squaws walk about with nothing on except a short petticoat. Consequently their whole "breast works" are open for inspections.

Of all the Indians that I have seen, both in Cala and on the "plains", I have met with but one who was stark naked. That was last summer. Two or three of us were up on the mountains some ten or fifteen miles beyond the settlements,

97

being out for the purpose of prospecting and having our dinner along, we were taking our morning, in a deep valley or gulch, alongside of an Indian trail. While resting under the shade of some tall pine trees, we heard a rumbling noise in the distance. Down the gulch, it came still nearer and finally, after winding up through the gulch and coming around a rock, we noticed a long string of Indians coming along in single file, about twenty-five in number including "squaws" and their "papusis" and some "ponies" upon the back of which some of the "squaws" and young ones were riding.

A few paces in front of the party was a tall Indian who was stark naked, and walking along as proud as a judge. When he passed us he looked at us and said, "How do, how do", which is a common word used among the Indians— expressive of their friendship for the pale faces, as white folks are generally termed by them.

I might recite many incidents in regard to Indians, but I will not take up anymore time here. Having been to town as above stated, I have the pleasure of announcing to you that I received your letter which was dated February 22nd, and the contents thereof are truly gratifying as I learn that you are all well and enjoying the comforts of this life and perhaps awaiting with eager expectation my speedy return home.

But that being the case, I must still keep you waiting for some time longer as I am not yet ready. I informed you in my last letter, two weeks since, that I would come home as soon as I could sell out. But I have formed another notion. The fact is I would like to raise a thousand dollars, ere I go home, besides what I need for passage money. I expect to raise that amount in the coarse of a few months. I am therefore inclined to think that I won't be home as soon as I was expecting to be. So you need not expect me for awhile yet. I will try and make up the sum of four hundred to send to you in my next letter, which will be about the first of May. You may therefore expect a letter with a draft in the beginning of June.

I have given you about all the particulars in my last letter including that of the six hundred dollars which I loaned out last summer. I also informed you of the intention

*of selling my cattle. I have not sold them, so I have no more
to say upon this subject at present.*

*I will now give you a few words in regard to the big
"lumps" of gold which were being taken out lately. Last
week I had the pleasure of seeing the largest piece of gold
that I ever saw or heard of being taken out of Cala.*

*This lump weighed twenty-four pounds and is worth five
thousand dollars. Such a piece is worth picking up and the
beauty of it is that one man alone found it. A few days
previous to this there were four men in company, all
Frenchmen but their claim would not pay anymore.
Consequently three of them left and went to another part of
the country. But one of them concluded to stay and work
awhile yet in hopes of making another strike. They had
been taking out considerable gold on several occasions in a
very short time. But, as is generally the case with
Frenchmen, when they have money, they first spent what
money they have accumulated before they go to work again.*

*In this case they had spent their money and were at
work again for several weeks without hardly making
enough to pay for their "grub", when they got disgusted with
their claim and left as above stated, while the other man
worked on several days longer.*

*In the morning of the day when he found the big piece,
he went around to his neighbors to beg his breakfast.
During the day he found the big lump and forty dollars in
fine gold, amounting altogether to about five thousand
dollars. I have seen the lucky fellow a few days afterward.
He was almost beside himself and hardly knew what he
was doing, so well he was pleased. But he said he won't
spend this money—that he would go home, which he did a
week afterward.*

*Such are the chances in California. There are more big
lumps deposited in the mountains throughout Cala, but it
requires much time and hard labor to find them. There are
millions of dollars worth of gold distributed around which
will never be found.*

*If you could see the large amount of labor which has
been done here in Cala for the last four years, you would be
astonished and think it almost impossible that so much
work would be accomplished in such a short space of time.*

But people here work in such good earnest. They dig down deep into the earth, level down hills, excavate mountains and turn rivers out of their proper courses for miles, in order to work in the bed of the river channel and everything else that comes in their way.

If they find nothing at one place, they try another. So we are constantly in hopes if we strike nothing today, we may tomorrow. Thus we are always laboring in good hopes. I have just as good an opinion of Cala now as I ever had so far as the gold digging is concerned. A person can make a good and easy living here. If I would make up my mind to stay here, I could make an easy and comfortable living. But, I do not intend to stay here. Consequently, I am not satisfied with a mere living.

This is generally the case with all of us, excepting those who have families here. If I had a family here, I would consider myself settled in this country. But unfortunately I have none, and am therefore discontented and will probably soon go in quest of one.

In answer to a question in your letter, whether I have any ladies here, I would state that I have none. But there are a great many women here—mostly all foreigners and of these the Chinese are the most numerous and the next in numbers are the Spanish, Mexicans and French, besides many other nations of smaller numbers.

There are not many American ladies here yet and those which are single are not of the right stripe. Consequently, I have nothing at all to do with them. I have not yet received nor given a kiss since I left the States, which is four years this month. So I have nothing more to say in regard to ladies at present.

A few more words in regard to our claim. We are sill taking out from thirty to fifty dollars per week to the hand, which is tolerable good wages and our prospects are good for making more and some day taking out a big lump. There is a probability as we have coarse gold in our claim which is a good sign. So we live and work in good hopes and probably die in despair as the old saying is. No more at present.

Hoping these lines may reach you all in the enjoyment of good health, as it leaves me. Write soon and give me all the news that has transpired in your neighborhood and send me some papers and Manheim papers if you can get any, as I had no news from that place for a long time.

I have sent you a paper most every month lately. My respects to you and all inquiring friends and to Mother in particular.

Yours truly,
D. B. Hackman

Chapter 22
The Worst End of the Bargain

Columbia, Tuolumne Co., Cala.
April 22ⁿᵈ, 1854

Dear Brother,

Once again, I take the pleasure of seating myself behind th old pine table, with pen in hand, to give you a few details in regard to California and also to inform you that I am still in the enjoyment of my usual good health.

I have not received a letter from you this last mail. I presume you are anxiously awaiting my return home and therefore did not write this mail. But, in that case, you will be disappointed, as you will perceive by these lines, that I am still among the gold diggers and doing very well—so well that we all give up the notion to go home this Spring. Our prospects for making money are better now than they have been any time heretofore. Our neighbors adjoining us are taking it out on a large scale.

I would have sold out for the last month or so previous for five hundred dollars, but at present I would not like to sell for less than double that amount. However, it is not likely that I will get that sum, nor do I care to sell. If it is worth that to others, it will pay me to stay here a little while longer.

I will now give you a few words in regard to this draft which you will find enclosed in this letter and which you will please get cashed as soon as possible and send me an answer thereof as soon as convenient. I would here state that two hundred dollars of this money is what I received for my two yoke of oxen, which I brought up from the valley last week and disposed of for two hundred and twenty-five dollars. I had them on a "rancho" pasture as stated. That is part of the six hundred dollars which I loaned out. Whether I get any more out of the gentleman is more than I am able to say at present, but as I have not explained to you heretofore how it happened that I loaned this man so much money, I would here state that this man whose name is Cuningham, came across the plains with us and when the company split up or divided on the plains as stated, this man stayed behind in company with others. While Mr. Kline and I were traveling along by ourselves and within a few days travel of California, this man overtook us when we were both out of money and out of provision. After learning of us, the condition that we were in, he kindly offered us the loan of as much money as we needed to reach California.

We gladly accepted his kind offer and thanked him very much for his timely aid, soon after which he left us and went on ahead. A few weeks after our arrival in Cala, I came across him one day and paid him back his money, soon after which I lost sight of him and did not meet him for three years.

One day last spring, I met him here on Yankee Hill. He was located here and had a large contract with a party to furnish them with saw logs at their mill. Everything looked prospering with him. One day he asked me for the loan of the amount and in return he gave me his note, a wagon and three yoke of oxen for security.

But about three weeks after this, I heard that he had failed and all his stock taken away except two yoke of oxen. It appears that the party who owned the mill had furnished or advanced him the stock or money. He had altogether ten yoke of oxen, three truck wagons, two drivers besides himself. Three yoke of oxen he owned which he had made over to me, but when he failed, one of his hands stole one yoke to save himself and hid them somewhere in the mountains for a short time, after which he sold them, as I was told afterward. So that is the way the matter stands.

When I gave him the money, he did it as a favor because he also favored me at a time when I truly stood in need of one. So one favor is worth another, but I think I have rather the worst of the bargain. But it may all come right yet. I often see him and he always promises to pay me and says that I shall lose nothing by him. He is at present working in the mines, so I must abide my time. If he is successful I may get it and if not I won't.

So you will perceive by the above that I owed him a small debt and you will therefore form your own opinion about this subject. You need not look for me to come home yet as I will probably stay here this summer yet. Write me often and send me some papers. If you see Mother give her my love and tell her that I hope and expect to see her before very long.

With these remarks I will bring my letter to a close for the present, hoping to hear from you soon. May these lines reach you all in the enjoyment of good health. Give my respects to Brother Jacob and family and Uncle Isaac and Aunt Fany and to all inquiring friends, and accept a portion for yourself. Direct your letter as usual.

From your Brother,
D. B. Hackman

Chapter 23
Snow in the Mountains

Columbia, California
May 11ᵗʰ, 1854

Dear Brother,

I am once again under obligation to address you with a few lines to inform you that I am still at my old place of abode and everything goes progressingly so far. I am not yet ready to leave California as you will perceive in my last letter. I may as well stay here as long as I have any prospects to make anything as anywhere else. Therefore you need not look for me yet. I will give you due notice when I am ready.

I would also inform you that I have not received any letters for the last two mails. I am always anxious to hear from home, if it is only a line or two. I expect an answer from Uncle Isaac about next mail. We gone some States papers this morning which were dated April 4ᵗʰ. They generally reach us in one month after date but they are not so interesting to me as home papers but there is none sent out here from the interior towns, only from the principle cities. Therefore, I get no news from and about Lancaster County— but what you sent to me, which I must confess is not very often—especially in the paper line.

In regard to the draft which I sent you last letter. It ought to reach you two weeks sooner than this. If not, you will please let me know as soon as possible so that I may see to it. In regard to the weather, the rainy or rather the Winter season is about over and the hot days of Summer are again inclining upon us. We had quite a rain and snow storm on the sixth of this month. The mountain about half a mile up from us was covered with snow while the foot or base of the mountain where we were at work at the time, it was raining very hard and not a particle of snow to be seen. But snow doesn't last long in this part of the country—at no time except higher up on the mountains where snow can be seen the year round. This may seem strange to you, but the mountains are so very high that it is always cold and frosty the whole summer and when it is raining in the valleys it is snowing on the mountains.

In order that you may form a better idea in regard to the climate here, I would state that early last fall, one day it commenced to snow and it continued all day long and part of the night. Next day being Sunday we had about fifteen inches of snow and the sky again bright, clear and warm.

We started off to go to town which was distant a mile and a half. We had not yet at that time sufficient water to work our claim to our advantage. So we were in high spirits expecting to have plenty of water when the snow would go off. But when we had come about half way to town, which laid on considerable lower down than the place where we started, we found the snow to be only half as deep and by the time we reached town, there was no snow at all and in the evening, when we returned to our mountain home, the snow had all disappeared without giving us a drop of water. In fact, the ground was as dry as though it had been no snow. So you will perceive by this that the climate is varying very much in short distances. This may suffice for the present, I have been writing a letter to you most every mail for the last five months. No more, give my love to all inquiring friends.

Respectfully your Brother,
D. B. Hackman

Chapter 24
A Descriptive View of Cala

Columbia, Tuolumne Co., California
June 24th, 1854

Dear Brother,

Once again, after waiting a long time, I am happy to announce to you the reception of a letter from you dated May 6th and which I am happy to state reached me in my usual good health. Hoping these lines reach you all in the enjoyment of the same.

I have also the pleasure to inform you I received two Lancaster papers dated May 1st and 16th and also one Manheim paper of the same date. The news contained in those papers are truly highly interesting to me. I whiled away a few hours very pleasantly perusing the news of old Lancaster and Manheim. It is a long time since I received any home papers. You cannot imagine how highly we appreciate letters or papers when coming from our far distant homes, every word or line is news to us. We get States papers twice a month which cost us three dollars per month or twenty-five cents apiece, but we do not feel the same interest in reading them as we do in those from our native homes.

Further, in reply to your opinion in regard to Cala, which you seem to think if I had your opinion I would be home long ago, and as you think I could do as well or better in Lancaster County or any other place and not be deprived of the comforts of this life etc. Now in order to give you a descriptive view of Cala, I would here state that my opinion in regard to this country is quite different than yours. As to making money, I think I can make more here with less labor than I could in any part of the States that is by manual labor. As I expect to make a living by working whether here or in the States, I would for my part prefer this country to

107

make an easy comfortable living if that was all that a person wants to come here for—but that is not the case with us.

The object in coming to California was not merely to make a living. If that had been the case, California, at this time, would be quite a different State from what it is. If we as miners had been more contented and settled down more permanently, many of us would be better off than what we are.

But as a general thing, miners lived in a very unsettled state of mind the first few years, the cause of which has been the fact that they were a considerable extent disappointed in their fond anticipations in regard to accumulating a "big pile" in a short time. The calculation was to come here and make a fortune in a very short time and leave the country again.

The idea of coming here and shoveling up the gold by the bushel and without any hard labor is all nothing. This, of course, has been a great disappointment to most of them and which has the cause of them traveling around from one part of the country to another always in quest of better and richer mines.

This, however, is not so much the case anymore. Lately, miners are becoming more permanently settled. The gold mines are worked more extensively and to a better advantage and experience has also taught them that the gold mines are more substantial than what they at first thought to be. Consequently, miners are putting up snug little houses and shanties for themselves and those who have no wives, of course, must keep bachelor's hall.

Small plots of ground are also fenced in for gardening purposes. Fruit trees of many varieties are also planted and agriculture is also more extensively carried on so, in a very few years, I expect California will be a great country to produce grain, fruit and vegetables more than will be consumed in this country.

A few weeks ago, when I was down in the valley about thirty miles from where I had my cattle, I saw many wheat fields which looked splendid. I have seen one field which I was told was one and a quarter miles long and a mile wide —all in one patch. There are many other fields along this valley, but there are hundreds and even thousands of acres which are not under cultivation yet. I have seen a farmer today who informed me that they are cutting their grain and that he expects some of it will yield forty and some even fifty bushels to an acre. That, I think, is not so bad for California. This may suffice to give you some idea in regard to this country.

I will now make a few remarks in regard to myself. You need not expect me home before next fall. I have not made much money for the last two weeks, but that is nothing if we do not make much for one or two week. We can make it all up when we come to the right place again.

The weather at present is very fine and pleasant, not so warm as it is generally at this season of the year. Provision too is very cheap at present. Please write soon and send me some more papers. You may expect some from me this mail. Direct your letters as above. Give my respects to all.

From your Brother,
D.B. Hackman
To A.B. Hackman, Millport

Chapter 25
Yellow Boys

Columbia, California
August 27th, 1854

Dear Brother,

I am once more happy to inform you that I received two letters from you last night. One was dated June 18th and the other June 30th, 1854—both of which were duly appreciated and highly interesting. I had no letters from you for the last two months. I am glad however to learn that you are all well with the exception of Brother Jacob's wife. I am also enjoying my usual good health, so I have nothing to complain of at the present.

You make mention in your letter in regard to making hay —that you must work early and late and hard at that and only receive one dollar and twenty-five cents per day. That I must say is rather hard work for a small remuneration and, as you stated, if you would do the same amount of labor in my place digging gold you would be better satisfied. That is truly said, dear Brother, but you would not even need to work so hard if you were at my place. On the contrary our work is not so very hard, nor do we early and late and still make as you say, from eight to twelve dollars per day to the hand.

But some days I am even doing better. I have lately made as high as fifty and even sixty dollars per day, but that is not very often that we make so much as that. Yesterday being Saturday, we worked but half a day. We washed out over two hundred and ninety-seven dollars. We took out one little lump worth one hundred and fifty-four dollars. Those are some of the "Yellow Boys" which we like to take up but they are not very plentiful.

You will perceive by this that one day we may get nothing and perhaps the next day take out a considerable "pile". Such are the chance in Cala. A person don't know when he may make a big "strike". We are never certain of our days wages until our days work is completed. Some days we have much, some little, and some days nothing at all. But on an average I am doing quite well and have done so for the last three months.

Since I sent you that draft for five hundred dollars, I made just that amount clear of all expenses and besides I have a better prospect for making more than I had any time heretofore. If our claim holds out awhile longer at the present rate, I may yet retrieve some of my unfortunate mishaps which have overtaken me during my sojourn in this country. So, I think I shall hold on awhile yet at least as I have such a good prospect to make money. I think you will agree with me for staying here under the circumstances, instead of coming home and go to work making hay etc., for one dollar and twenty-five cents per day.

But, nevertheless, home is a dear name, and some days I feel a great desire to see home and friends once again. Why it is, I do not know, but of late I feel anxious about home. It is now nearly five years since I left home and friends behind me. That is a long time, and yet the time did not seem so very long to me either. But, if I live and keep my health, I expect to see home and friends sometime this fall if no preventing providence.

In your last letter of June 30th, I was happy to learn that you received my draft for that money. In regard to some questions in that letter, I will make no comments as most of them are embodied in the above letter. So I will curtail this letter somewhat as I have several more to write this morning —one to Manheim, not to my "Lady Love", but to A.J. Eby postmaster and one to my old friend and partner, Mr. Pinkham of St. Louis, Missouri, who sold out his share of our claim not long since for five hundred dollars and left for home.

It was he, as stated in a former letter, who owned the only china dish or plate to eat off of, which plate he made a present to me with instructions to take good care of it and not break or wash it too often for fear of wearing it out too soon. In the event of him coming back again, I was to return it to him again without blemish.

In regard to washing it too often, I said he need not be under any apprehension but as to breaking or other accidental causes, I could not be so positive. However, I said, I will take the very best of care.

In regard to my "Lady Love", as you would wish to know, I wrote several letters to her the first and second years of my sojourn in this country, but I never received an answer. So, I have no correspondence with her at all. I heard, however, through another source about a year ago, that she was still single. But, whether she had discarded me or sent me adrift, I am not able to say, but hope to the contrary.

How about the lady at the love feast who made inquiries about me? I presume she wishes me to give her a call on my return home, but I cannot exactly promise her that I shall. But you may at least give her my compliments. With these remarks I will bring my letter to a close, hoping to hear from you soon. If you see mother, tell her that I send my love and hope to see her before many months have past away.

Accept my kindest regards,

Your Brother,
D.B. Hackman

Chapter 26
Belzebub and Prostrate Monarchs

Columbia, California
September 30ᵗʰ, 1854

Dear Bro,

Another month has past away without a letter from you. Yesterday being Sunday, I went to town expecting to receive a letter from you, but there was none. Instead, I received a lot of papers from Manheim and Lancaster and one New York paper sent by J.N. Ensminger, Printer, and A.J. Eby, Postmaster, all of which were highly appreciated and truly interesting to me. I have no very encouraging news to write to you. Our claim is not yielding anything more than ordinary wages this while past and besides I feel more depressed in spirits now that I did at anytime since I am in the country, especially since my partner Mr. Pinkham left, which is now nearly three months.

At the time when he left, he thought he might probably come back again this fall. That, he would let me know as soon as he got home, but I had no letter from him yet. So, I do not know what his intentions are. If I thought he would soon come back again, I might probably stay awhile yet, but according to my present views of the matter, I think I shall leave the country very soon.

Life in California has no charms for me anymore and especially "Pork and Beans". I might almost exclaim like the miner who lamented his fate and sang the following lines:

High on a rough and dismal crag
Where Keane might spout – aye there's the rub,
Where oft, no doubt, some midnight hag,
Had danced a jig with Belzebub,

There stood beneath the pale moonlight,
A miner grim with visage long,
Who vexed the drowsy ear of night,
With dreadful thyme and dismal song.

He sang – I have no harp or lute,
We sound the stern decrees of Fate,
I once possessed a two-holed flute,
But that I sold to raise a stake.

Then wake they strains, my wild tin pan,
Afright the crickets from their lairs,
Make wood and mountain ring again –
And terrify the grizzly bears.

My home is on a distant shore,
My gentle love is far away,
She dreams not that my trousers are tore,
And all besmeared with dirty clay.

She little knows how much, of late,
Amid these dark and dismal scenes,
I've struggled with an adverse fate,
And lived, oh Lord! On pork and beans!

Oh, that a bean would never grow,
To fling its shadows o'er my heart –
My tears of grief are hard to flow,
But food like this must make then start.

The good old times have passed away,
And all things now are strange and new,
All save my shirt and trousers grey,
Three stockings and one cowhide shoe.

Oh! Give me back my days of yore,
And all those bright, though fading scenes,
Connected with that happy shore,
Where turkeys grow, and claims and greens.

Those days that sank, long weeks ago,
Deep in the solemn, olden times,
And left no trace that man may know,
Save trousers all patched up behind.

And boots all tore, and shirt all tore,
Or botched up with most outrageous stitches,
Oh give me back the days of yore,
And my best go-to-meeting britches.

The above is a tolerable correct representation of us miners in general. But you need not infer from this that I denounce California as a poor country to live in. On the contrary, I think it is one of the most pleasant countries to live in and the most healthy too. In regard to money, I have never seen a place where people feel more independent than here because every one seems to have plenty of shining "rocks".

In regard to the mines, they are pretty well worked over —especially in the gulches and ravines and surface diggings. But, there are millions upon millions of dollars deposited in these hills and mountains, much of which will eventually be taken out, but will require much labor and a great deal more capital. But, many of the present inconveniences will be overcome by and by when labor and provisions become cheaper, which I presume will not be very long because, in a very few years, there will be more grain, fruit, and vegetables raised than will be consumed in this country.

There is no place in the whole Union that can compete with Cala in vegetables or big trees either. I have seen common potatoes which measured nearly a foot in length and weighed six pounds. I have also seen accounts of the following articles: - squashes that weigh 120 pounds, onions 22 inches in circumference weight 6 pounds, beets 18 inches long weight 51 pounds, and sweet potatoes 20 pounds, carrots 10 pounds. This may seem almost incredible to you but it may nevertheless be true as I have seen some very large vegetables myself up here in the mines.

115

In regard to trees, there are several groves of large trees here. The Mariposa is the largest and finest. There are two hundred which are more than 12 feet in diameter and fifty more than 16 feet and six more than 30 feet. But the largest, called the Prostrate Monarch, now lying on the ground, and believed to have fallen fully one hundred and fifty years ago, but enough is remaining to show that with the bark on it had been forty feet thick.

The Prostrate Monarch

Figures give little idea of such dimensions. Measure up forty feet on a house wall, then four hundred feet along the ground and try to picture the diameter and height of the Prostrate Monarch as it stood a thousand years ago.

Many of these trees are from three to four hundred feet long. There is another grove of large trees in Calaveras County about twenty-five miles from our place. I have conversed with some men who were there only a few days ago, who informed me there were over a hundred of these large trees in a circumference of about fifty acres. The largest of these trees measures ninety-five feet around it, the bark of which is one and a half feet thick. One of the trees had been blown off about two hundred feet above the ground, around the trunk of which a party went to work and put up steps or stairs from the ground up on top of which there is a large platform with a railing around for which twenty five cents is charged for coming up stairs on this platform.

One of these trees was cut down, which required the labor of five men, twenty five days before they got it down. After it was down, they took the bark off in strips of twelve feet long and shipped them to San Francisco where they had them set up and made a saloon to take refreshments, just for the novelty of the thing.

This grove of trees is about fifteen miles from the nearest settlement up on the mountains, but a party of men went to work and put up a large hotel and another is in course of erection.

They made a road from the mines up and have stages running upon them daily. There are hundreds of people upon the ground daily from all parts of California. Thus you will perceive that California is a great country to produce "giants". In fact everything is gigantic here, even little "babies" are giants, as I have seen some very tall ones.

But I have nothing more to say of giants. So I will, with a few more remarks, bring this letter to a close. I may probably be on my way home by the time that you receive this letter. If I can make arrangements to dispose of my claim, I may leave in about two weeks which would be the middle of October. But, you may at least expect another letter when I get to San Francisco, so no more at present. If you see mother tell her that I have for once made up my mind to come home.

My love and respects to you all,

Your Brother,
D.B. Hackman

Chapter 27
A True and Honorable Heart

David informs his romantic interest back home that he plans to return.

Columbia, California
October 4th, 1854

Miss Miller,

Excuse me for thus addressing you, but as I have not as yet had any letters from you since I been in California, I am at a loss how to address you. Whether any news from me will be acceptable to you or no is unknown to me. All that I wish to acquaint you of is that I am about to leave California to return home. By the time that you receive this I shall be in New York, or Philadelphia. But before I come to Manheim, I should wish to have you send me a few lines to Lancaster that I may know whether I am a welcome visitor to you or not. I should be happy to call on you first, if it may please you of my doing so. I would furthermore state that, if ever I have the honor of meeting you, I can meet you with a true and honorable heart, be assured of that. With these few lines I will come to close, hoping that in a very short time I may, from him who loves but one, have the honor of seeing you.

yours – truly – yours

DB. Hackman

Chapter 28
The End of My Wanderings

David prepares to leave for home.

San Francisco, California
October 7ᵗʰ, 1854

Dear Brother,

Having reached the end of my wanderings here in California, I am about to set my face eastward towards my home and friends, beyond the dark blue ocean, which seems doubly dear to me, when I recall to mind that far-off land, and anticipate under providence a speedy reunion with you all

On the fifth Ints., I left my claim and friends on Yankee Hill. The claim I made over to a friend of mine, who is to pay me a certain amount if it pays and if not, there is not much lost. I left the Hill in the morning and went to Columbia accompanied by some of my partners and other friends, who wanted to see me off.

On my arrival at this place, I received a letter of my old friend Mr. Pinkham, who stated that he was on his way back to Cala and would probably reach San Francisco in the middle of this month and that I should engage a boarding house or a shanty where he could move in till he could further provide for himself and family, as he is accompanied by his wife and four children.

Shortly after he got home, he told his wife that he could not stay there and would go back to California. His wife said she too would go, so they sold out and left for the land of Gold in less than three weeks after his arrival home.

I was almost tempted to stay and return again to the old home on the Hill. But after second thought, I concluded to go to San Francisco as I may probably meet him there.

So I told my partners and friends to provide a place for him, which they readily promised to do as they were glad for his return to the mines.

At four o'clock P.M. I took leave of my friends and my associates, and bid farewell to the mines and was soon whirled along in a coach at a rapid rate over dusty hills to Sonora, a distance of eight miles, where we arrived at half-past five. Here I had to lay over till next morning.

Sonora is considered one of the most important inland towns in the state. It was incorporated as a city in 1851 and is nicely laid out in wide streets and contains about four thousand inhabitants. There are several large commodious hotels, and a good proportion of other substantial, both public and private buildings. Sonora is situated on the north branch of the Tuolumne River, Tuolumne County, about sixty-five miles north-east from Stockton, and is called the metropolis or capital of the Southern Mining region.

About two years ago, I was present at the great fire which occurred here when the whole town, together with the greater part of stock, goods, furniture and everything else was consumed in less than four hours. Not a house was standing, except quite a small portion at one end of the town and a few shanties along the outskirts. Many frame buildings were torn down and the rubbish carried to one side for the purpose of staying the progress of the fire, but the fire would soon over leap the intervening space and continue on its course right and left as long as there was a building within reach of the devouring element.

This town has only shared the same fate, like many others, which were partially and in many cases wholly destroyed by fire.

On the following morning, October sixth, at three A.M. I took a seat with the driver on a mail coach, to which were attached six spirited horses, which were soon taking us along at a tolerable rate, up hill, and down steep and sloping mountains and through beautiful valleys toward Stockton, where we arrived at three P.M. We passed many towns, and smaller villages on the way, but of little note.

Stockton is situated on the northeastern shore of one of the "sloughs" of the San Joaquin River, about three miles from the main channel of the river. Its population numbers *about three thousand but the buildings in this place are quite inferior to those of Sonora.*

The river for light steamers and vessels is navigable as far as this city and its central location between the Southern Mining region and the coast, will ultimately secure to it a large and increasing trade.

At five o'clock P.M. I embarked on a steamer for San Francisco which was soon gliding along on its smooth but sluggish waters. The greater portion of the valley along this river lies very low, and is therefore subject to inundation once or twice a year which renders farming or other agricultural pursuits unprofitable along the greater part of this river.

Having made the passage during the night between Stockton and San Francisco, I am not able to give any further description along this route. At 3 A.M. on the following morning we arrived at the metropolis of Cala, distant from Stockton one hundred miles.

Chapter 29
The Metropolis of Cala

David's letter continues...

Passengers did not leave the steamer until daylight, after which I went up town in company with others. I put up at a second class hotel, on Pacific Street. After breakfast, I took a stroll through town. I have read and heard much of this great town and have seen progress made in other parts of this state. But this casts far into the shade all of the progress or improvements that I have yet seen.

I was very much surprised to see so large a number of massive buildings which adorn many of the streets of this city, and in architectural beauty, many of them will compare favorably with those devoted to similar purposes at any of the Eastern cities. Nor does it lack in business, if I may infer from the crowds on the sidewalks, the rattle of drays, the display of hacks, the roll of omnibuses, the ringing of bells, the fruit stand on the corners, the various peddlers of small wares, the long wharves loaded with merchandise, and the spacious harbor dotted all over and alive with the shipping of every clime.

All these are sufficient evidence of the energy and thrift of this great city, the origin of which might be covered with the dusts of time, because it is but in the fifth year of its existence. During that short space of time the whole city was made once, and several times partially destroyed by fire. The first of which occurred in May 1851 and extended east and west from DuPont to Battery Street, and north and south from Broadway to Pine Street including sixteen entire squares and parts of four others, involving a loss of about ten million of dollars. Another occurred about seven weeks after this which consumed eight whole squares and parts of seven others, including several new churches, the city hall, and hospital, estimated loss three million dollars. Several other fires occurred since but of less magnitude.

There are erected on almost every street a number of fireproof buildings consisting of stone and iron, which will largely contribute to check the spreading of that destructive element in the future. The city has one principle plaza or public ground called Portsmouth Square, situated in the central part of the city, and several others at more remote points.

The streets are narrow and intersect at right angles, about forty extending from the bay westward over the hills, and about twenty north and south. The principal business streets lying in that direction are Front, Battery, Sansome, Montgomery, DuPont, Kearney and Powell Streets, and those lying east and west are Vallejo, Broadway, Pacific, Jackson, Washington, Clay, Commercial, Pine, Rush, Sutter and Market Streets.

The principal public wharves are Market, Central, Pacific and Broadway, besides these there are three or four private wharves. The city hall is a large and stately edifice fronting on Portsmouth Square and is one hundred and fifty feet deep by one hundred broad, enclosing a spacious court and is constructed of brick and faced on the front with dark gray stone. This is nicely fitted up and furnished for the accommodation of the state and city courts and the various public offices.

There are eighteen churches in the city of various denominations, several of which are tasteful specimens of architectural skill. There are three public and several private markets in the city and none in the world are more abundantly supplied with all the necessaries or with a greater variety of the luxuries of this life.

Newspapers, there are printed in this city twelve daily papers, two tri-weeklies, six weeklies, one commercial, one French, and one Sunday paper. In addition to the above enumerations, there are a great many manufacturing establishments of various kinds all through the city, the suburbs of which already resemble those of older towns.

Several long streets running out to the bay on the lower sections of town, are now lined with spacious warehouses and other stores, some of which are constructed of brick and others of stone or iron. No longer than two years ago, the angry waves of the bay were lashing the strand as far up into the city as Montgomery Street, and now there are four broad avenues and several alleys lying between the original limit and the present water line. The labor and energy required for this improvement in so short a time appears almost incredible, but it is nevertheless true.

San Francisco truly is a great city. Here are people from all nations and of different languages and in consequence of the many adventurers who congregate here, a great many gambling houses, drinking saloons, theaters, and other houses of low repute have sprung up in every section of the city, all of which are excessively patronized and among the prevailing evils are gambling, intemperance, and licentiousness.

Having thus given you an inadequate description of the rise and progress of this city, by which you may form a partial idea of its greatness, the foundation of which was laid only six years ago, and now contains over fifty thousand inhabitants, and during that time it has twice been almost totally destroyed by fire and once partially, but in each case it has again reappeared almost magically, as it was.

Previous to the year 1848, the whole territory now covered by the city, contained only about ten or fifteen small buildings. In May 1848 the first gold discoveries were made in California, through the agency of General John A. Sutter, who emigrated from Missouri across the plains to Oregon in the year 1839, and in 1840 he came over to California where he located himself in the great valley of Sacramento, near where the great City of Sacramento is now located.

Here he erected for himself a kind of a fort or walled mansion. The laborers employed by him were chiefly Indians, whom he trained to the knowledge and skill of the various branches of labor. Here he resided for many years, devoting his time principally to farming and raising stock, etc.

In 1847 he conceived the idea of erecting a sawmill on the American River, about forty miles east from his residence, where there was good water power and any quantity of the best kind of timber. This mill was finished early in 1848, but in order to expedite their work in opening the discharging or tail race, they turned on a powerful stream of water into a small ditch or sluice way opened for that purpose and thus in a short time, washed away a large quantity of earth, carving a broad deep channel.

After stopping off the water, they inspected the work of their exploit and discovered along the bottom of this newly-made channel or race, many shining particles, and believing them to be gold, collected a quantity and communicated the intelligence to their employer Mr. Sutter, who after examining and subjecting it to some strong acids, pronounced it to be gold.

After further examination, they soon ascertained that the shores and the bed of the south fork of that river were rich in deposits of gold. In the meantime other persons were watching the movements of these gentlemen, who also made search with equal success and thus the great discovery soon became generally known, and hundreds of native Californians from the southern portion wended their way towards the streams, gorges, and mountains of the north and east.

Soon the golden news reached the Atlantic States, and "on the wings of the wind", it was wafted throughout the whole world. A large emigration immediately set in and wended their way towards the land of gold.

Thus California has become the great state which it now has reached, and is but yet in its infancy. Three days after my arrival in the city, I took a trip up the bay to Alveso in Santa Clara County distant from the city fifty miles, by request of A.J. Eby, Manheim, who stated in a letter to me a few months ago, that he has an old bachelor uncle living near Alveso and if convenient, I should hunt him up. Therefore by way of pastime, which by the way does not seem to be wafted on the wings of the wind since my arrival here, and the time set for the departure of the steamer which is to sail on the 16th Ints.

Therefore I took passage on a little steamer plying between this city and Alveso, for which passage I paid three dollars and dinner included, arriving at about 4 PM at the little village of Alveso, which is situated at the head of the bay.

After making inquiries here in regard to old uncle whose name is Lick, I was informed that he lived within two and a *half miles of this place. After taking the road pointed out to me I soon reached the place but on my arrival I was informed that he went to the city and would not be home for a day or two.*

A young cousin, however, of Eby's was here and entertained me quite agreeably and invited me to stay as long as I wished to remain. I ascertained through him that Mr. Lick, who is also this young man's uncle, was very wealthy. The farm upon which he resides contains about six hundred acres principally all under cultivation. Besides this, he has erected a large mill three and a half stories height at a cost of two hundred thousand dollars.

He employs from twenty to thirty-five hands the year round. Farmers in this country have no barns. They haul their grain on large heaps or stacks in the fields, after which they thrash it out and burn the straw. They have no women on this place. They have three Frenchmen employed to do the culinary affairs. On the following morning, I took leave of the Lick farm, and went back to the city again, where I arrived in the evening, being the eleventh. Having ascertained that no steamers had arrived from the States, during my absence,I went to my hotel for the night.

On the following morning after breakfast, I went out and in looking down the street, I was agreeably surprised to see one of my late partners, who had just come out of the hotel where he was stopping and was looking around and wondering where he could find me. I hailed him and was really very glad to see him, because I was very lonesome.

He informed me that he sold out for one hundred dollars, and came on to San Francisco, intending to go home in the same steamer with me. We tramped about the city all day, amusing ourselves as best we could, but we spent the greater part of the day along the wharves, in anticipation of the arrival of the steamers containing our friend.

But the day past off and night came on, without the glad tidings of hearing the cannons boom, announcing the arrival of mail steamer, which is customary on entering a port to fire off a cannon.

Having nothing more to look for, we went back to our respective hotels, took supper, after which we went out again. But this time, we went around to visit some of the big gambling houses, which at this time of night were in full blast.

During this day, and the greater part of the night, these houses are thronged with the old and young who drink and stake their money on the wheel of fickle fortune and occasionally win, but are often beggared. Some of these houses contain from six to ten tables and upon each of the tables is placed a pile of gold and silver coin, amounting to from one up to five thousand dollars, which is denominated their "bank".

Sometimes these banks are busted, that is, a person betting against them having, using the gamblers phrase, "a streak of extraordinary good luck", will win all the money on the table. Many of the tables are in charge of ladies, "who are in the service of the proprietor", and who are richly clad in satins and silks, who smile invitingly at everyone, and wave gracefully her hand, sparkling with diamonds and gold, as an invitation for persons to be seated and to try their luck and win her pile or lose their own.

The "green one" who yields to the fascinations of these fair "tempters", will surely be deprived of his golden strength, especially if he is not "proof against the ardent" which is handed around freely. Having been lookers-on, like hundreds of others, we turned our steps towards our hotels for the night.

On the following morning after breakfast we went out again, wandering through this "Babel" City, which may truly be termed by that name, on account of the many languages which are spoken here. After ascertaining that no steamer had arrived from the States, during the night, we visited a portion of the city which is principally inhabited by Chinese. The city is full of them, but they have their separate sports among themselves and are great gamblers too.

Indeed, it is scarcely more natural for a Chinaman, Spaniard, Mexican or Chilean to eat, then to gamble. It is nothing strange to see them squatted down on the sidewalks to gamble. Having reached the particular locality in which the Chinese dwell, and congregate in large numbers, in small dark rooms in which they eat, drink spirits, smoke opium and have their sport, in various kinds of games – all foreign to us.

The characteristics of the Chinese enables the curious who go among them and learn their manners, customs, trades, habits, virtues and vices, almost as well and satisfactorily as they could be learned on a visit to their own country.

These people are very friendly, sociable, and are pleased to explain all their customs and practices, for the improvement of the curious. The next great object worthy of note is the grading of the streets which is another stupendous improvement among others. I noticed one street now in progress of grading, which is at least thirty feet deep and not only the streets but the buildings and lots are excavated and the earth is hauled into the lower parts of other streets, which I have seen filled up level with the first story of houses. To those buildings excavated is added another story underneath, making a two story building three stories high, or otherwise as the case may be. I have seen both frame, and brick buildings thus excavated.

I might enumerate many objects which would be interesting to you, but time will not admit of writing anymore today. Having extended our walk through different portions of the City, and finally along the wharves but without the arrival of the object for which we are looking, returned to our hotels.

On the following morning being Sunday, I arose early and went down to the wharf before breakfast to learn whether our looked-for steamer had come in, but none had come, so went back to my hotel. After breakfast I joined my companion at his hotel. After consulting awhile what to do to pass the day, which being our last day of our stay here, and the time seemed to drag around slowly. After our consultation we concluded to go down to the wharves but we soon got tired there, so we returned and went uptown again. We felt about as restless as two beings could feel.

About nine o'clock all the bells were ringing, the streets were crowded with people going and coming from different directions. Many going to hear the Gospel preached to them, but by far the greater portion found their way into the gambling and drinking saloons, or theaters, and other

128

places of amusements which were open here on Sundays as well as week days without distinction.

We too were among the latter number, but we excused ourselves for non attendance at church, on account of our restlessness. Having extended our rambles through town to different places of amusements until about ten o'clock PM when we were about returning to our hotel, we heard some newsboys who came running up from the direction of the wharves calling our late papers for sale, "just arrived from New York, New Orleans, Boston and St. Louis", we started off double quick down to the wharf.

When we reached the place everything was confusion. The wharf was crowded with hacks, drays, and omnibuses, and hundreds of people. We looked around quickly for our friend, but not seeing him, I told my companion to keep watch on the wharf while I made my way with difficulty over the planks laid from the wharf onto the boat. As many more were in quest of similar object that I was, keeping the planks perfectly champed up.

Having reached the boat, I looked it all through but in vain. My friend had either gone ashore or did not come in this boat, which by this time was nearly deserted by passengers. So, I went ashore, which was still crowded. I called my companion by name several times but without receiving an answer.

Thinking that he went back to his boarding place, I too started and went up town, slowly, feeling very much, both discouraged and disappointed, for not seeing my friend. On my way I stopped in at my companion's hotel. In answer to my inquiries I was told that he had not yet come in, so I left to go to my hotel.

When I reached that place I was surprised to see the room crowded with people and almost the first persons that I saw were my companion and long looked-for friend, who looked as hale and hearty as ever. After a hearty shaking of hands and a few commonplace remarks, he gave us a brief description of his trip home and back again. And says he, "Here I am with my wife and four little ones", and reaching in his pocket he drew out a fifty cent piece. "This", he said, "is all the money that I have to my name, and two hundred miles yet to travel before reaching the mines."

But", says he, "I have a friend with me who will see me through." He was no less glad to see me than I was to see him, although he said he would rather have met me up in the mines than here. I told him I got home sick after he left me, so I concluded to go home. He really felt very sorry on account of my leaving and I believe if I had not purchased my ticket, for which I paid one hundred and fifty dollars steerage passage, cabin passage being three hundred dollars, I should have returned again, but as it was, I could not. As it was late in the night, we retired for the present.

On the following morning, after breakfast, our friend introduced us to his wife, who received us very cordially as friends of her husband and after a short talk with her asking and answering questions on various topics we took our final leave of her as our time was now limited.

Nine o'clock being the time set for all passengers to be on board the steamer, therefore we must make preparations for our departure. Our friend is going to see us on board. I brought a pair of blankets along which our friend assures us are not of much account on the trip, so I made him a present of them.

I will close this letter and have it mailed, as it will go in the same steamer with me, but it may reach you a few days in advance of me.

This closes my career in the land of Gold.

D. B. Hackman

Chapter 30
Journal of my Voyage
from San Francisco to New York

David describes his experiences aboard a steamship to the Isthmus of Panama and onward to New York.

The SS Golden Gate: built in 1851

October 16th, 1854

Eleven o'clock A.M. we took leave of our friend, and went aboard the steamer "Golden Gate", which is a large and noble ship, staunch, airy and commodious in all her arrangements. She is well officered and manned and carries between eight and nine hundred passengers on this trip. Her accommodation capacity is one thousand but she has at one time brought up from Panama, fourteen hundred passengers.

We have on board this steamer about one hundred and fifty passengers, who started out two weeks ago, but the steamer that went out with was wrecked about twenty-four hours sail down the coast, within four or five miles of the shore. No lives were lost but the steamer was a total wreck, with all the freight and most of the passengers' effects. The steamer belonged to a company running an opposition line between this and Panama, but that trip was to be the last of the opposition line, because the Pacific Mail Steamship company bought them off and put the fare up again to the present high rates. The fare from here to New York for the last month or two was as low as fifty dollars a trip.

Consequently when those wrecked passengers came back to San Francisco, they found the company's office closed and could not recover their passage money and many of them perhaps not having enough money to pay another passage and others perhaps feeling rather timorous to risk another trip so soon, may have deemed it provident to go back into the mines again.

Having been detained longer than the time set for the departure of the steamer, we did not get off until after noon, owing "as I understand" to an Express Company which had been detained in delivering its freight of gold.

At two o'clock P.M. all were on board, and the cannon's voice gave the final signal for departure. Orders were issued to make loose the chains, and haul in the planks, which order was complied with in double quick. The steamer slowly rounded on her course down the bay. In a very short time the crowd which had assembled on the wharf to witness our departure, were no more to be seen from the steamer and soon the Magic City itself was lost to view behind the high and rocky cliff that forms the south eastern shore of the "Golden Gate", so termed on account of the narrow rocky point in the bay.

Slowly and cautiously the steamer finds her way among the rocks that obstruct the passage between the city and the ocean. One by one, the crags and hills, and vales, that line the shore are lost in the distance, until about seven o'clock, no part of the "Golden Land" is visible except the summit of "Old Diablo", towering in gloomy grandeur among the clouds which play around the summit. Soon even that lofty mountain has disappeared, and California, with all its vastness, its wonderful past, and its mighty future, is again distant land to me.

The novelty of the passing scenes on board soon occupied my mind. I turned to take a view of the steamer

132

and the multitude who are to be my companions in perils and hopes for many days, all of whom are strangers to me except my companion, who, like myself, enjoys the scenes around us which were magnificent to behold at this hour, just at night-fall. All points of the shore had faded from our view. No objects were visible but the steamer "Golden Gate", the clear and arching sky, the shoreless ocean, and the reflection of the evening sun, sinking in golden splendor into her ever-restless bosom. Yielding to the power of the enchantment, as night closed around the contemplative scene, we retired to our "ocean-rocked bunks", and bid a silent adieu to all.

Chapter 31
A Description of the Steamer *Golden Gate*

October 17th, 1854

Left my berth at early dawn, went on deck to get a fresh and cool saltwater bath. The weather is fine, the sea calm, the sky bright and clear and just enough breeze to fill the ship's canvas, which is making good headway under the combination of both steam and sail.

Land is in sight but at a considerable distance, which is piled up in irregular heights of several hundreds of feet against the sky and appears in beautiful contrast with the dark blue water of the ocean. The summit has a darkish fringe, which resembles vegetation, but the view is so distant that objects become obscure and cannot be distinguished with certainty.

In the absence of any other objects worthy of none, and in order to expedite the monopoly of the day, I will give a brief description of our steamer and the order in which it is governed.

The "Golden Gate", as already stated, is a large and commodious ship. She carries one thousand passengers with ease and comfort to all. The length of her deck is three hundred and twenty-five feet, which affords a splendid promenade, which may be seen by the passengers availing themselves of the opportunity thus afforded, by marching around in an oblong circle in a continuous string, especially after supper in the cool of the evening.

Steerage passengers have not the same privilege accorded to them, as cabin passengers have, because those belonging to the forecastle are prohibited to enter upon the domains of the cabin passengers. But the latter may, if they choose, come over on our side, where they will be treated according to their behavior. Midway of the deck is the dividing line. There are three classes of passengers, first and second cabin and steerage.

The first take their meals with the captain and officers, and the second take their meals after them at the same table. But the steerage passengers have their separate department and take their meals standing, which consists principally of corn beef and salt pork with beans and other soup twice a week. All of the tables on ship board are suspended from the ceiling, which are swinging constantly according to the ship's motion.

Our quarters on this steamer are quite comfortable, tidy, and well ventilated. In fact so far as I have seen, all of the compartments, including steerage, cabins, engine room, kitchen, bakery, butcher shops, are clean as a drawing room. Plates, knives and forks, and spoons are shining and everything in proper order. The great steamer might appropriately be termed a floating palace. Live cattle are carried along to supply the tables as they are wanted, for cabin use only.

The voyager of this steamer cannot but admire the order and system, which prevail among the officers and crew. The government has its Judicial and financial departments, each distinct, but all subject to the Captain who is absolute monarch of the ship.

The common sailors are under the control of the first and second mates. The latter also take the captain's comment in their order, if he is absent but the captain holds them responsible for any disorder among the sailors and gives no personal attention to the latter.

The engineers have the control of the engine and the speed of the vessel, and all firemen. The purser is treasurer, receives and disburses all the moneys, provides the supplies, and keeps accounts and "reckoning" of the ship.

The steward is the head, and chief lord of the kitchen, and dining rooms. All the cooks and waiters are his subjects. The passengers, especially steerage passengers, regard these functionaries with peculiar interest, because they will sometimes, through their generosity, procure a good morsel to eat. But they regard the passengers precisely according to the length of their purse-strings and the kind of knot into which it is twisted. They all have a strong dislike to the hard knot, but smile complacently at the bow-knot which opens easily.

The watch also is a very important and responsible office under the direction of the mates. The twenty-four hours are divided into a certain number of watches, four are always on duty at the same time. In sailor's phrase "they are four on and four off", which is changed every four hours. Each change of the watch is announced by the loud peel of a large bell mounted upon the forecastle.

Night is again closing around us. The coast is yet in sight but at a considerable distance and we are fast receding from it. The day has been bright and clear, and just enough breeze stirring to make it comfortable. Thus I close my journal for today.

Chapter 32
A Limitless Expanse of Liquid Glass

October 18ᵗʰ, 1854

This morning left my pillow at five. No, not my pillow, as that is a commodity which steerage passengers are not provided with or any other bed clothing. We are only provided with a frame six by two, over which is stretched canvas. Having left my blankets back, I am therefore without any bed clothing and but my coat for a pillow. So I should have said, I left my bedless cot at five this morning and went up on deck.

The morning was bright and clear, not a cloud to be seen, "not even as large as a mans hand", is visible in the horizon which blends in the misty distance with the deep-blue surface of the ocean. Such a surface, so calm and smooth, not a breeze to ruffle it; too broad, pure and bright, it looks like a mirror, radiant with the reflection of the morning sun, just rising out of the deep blue ocean in the distance.

One of the distinguishing characteristics of the Pacific is this calm surface. It will often last, as I am informed by one of the old 'Tars', for several hours, especially in the morning, when it looks like a limitless expanse of liquid glass. Its motion is then sluggish and heavy, like molten metal. To this appearance its name is attributed, though they are less violent and destructive than those of the Atlantic.

When we are favored by breezes or winds, they generally blow in the night but are back to their sources on the land before morning.

This day has been very still, and uninteresting on board. No land is in sight, nor have we seen a sail or steamer since we left port. We are approaching the locality known by seafaring men as the Pacific Whaling Ground, but at this time nothing is visible but the monotonous scene of sky, water, and our steamer. The heat during the day has been rather oppressive and the passengers have generally lounged about, lazily on the shady side of the decks. Some amusing themselves by playing all-fours, some reading novels and others sleeping.

The steamer, at noon today, has made the preceding forty-eight hours 513 miles, thus bringing us 513 miles from the port of an Francisco and with this I will close my record for today and try to find repose in my downy – no, I mean upon my bed on canvas.

Chapter 33
Gone Like the Baseless Fabric of a Vision

October 19th, 1854

This morning I got awake rather earlier than usual. I was uncomfortably disturbed by the motion of the steamer, which was rocking me upon my cot, back and forth, precisely like a cradle, which put me in mind of rocking the "babies", and deeming myself rather too tall a "baby" to be rocked.

I got up and went on deck. The sky was overcast with dark heavy clouds and the wind was blowing in fitful gusts from the northwest and is angrily throwing the white and briny spray completely over the bow of the ship, which rolls and pitches and trembles from stem to stern.

But the good old steamer bears herself manfully in the conflict with her bowsprit pointed towards her true course. She plows her rapid way onward, regardless of the war of the elements, though the heavy swells heave her high up in the air or she settles deep into the trough of the ocean. Yet she deviates not from her course, but minds her helm and proves her fidelity by the air-line course which she pursues.

I have great confidence in the old steamer, which is pounding through the waves like a seagull, and feel that under the guidance of providence, she will bear us safely on our journey and reach her destined port.

After reaching the deck of the steamer and taking a survey of the disturbed elements around us, I could not help but think: "Oh how fickle is thy serenity; when last I bade thee good night, thy face was bright and smooth, not a line of disquiet was on it, not a breath disturbed its repose. Surrounded by the glories of a lovely evening, unnumbered twinkling stars, the full-orbed moon, the pallid silver sky, all shone forth in full glory as I had taken my leave, on the previous evening. The morning has appeared, but where are thy evening charms? Gone like the baseless fabric of a vision."

We have now reached the influence of the blows and rough seas which are coming in and along the Gulf of California. This gulf is affected by the land winds from the north, east and west, and increase sometimes to considerable storms. We will be in them for a day or two. The swells roll heavily which appear like ascending a steep hill, then down again into a deep hollow, or trough of perhaps several acres in extend—the waves and swells appearing high above us all around. The steamer rocks and heaves and rolls side-wise and rises and falls almost at the same time.

Soon after breakfast, many of the passengers began to show decided evidence of an uneasiness, peculiar to a large majority of freshmen on ship board and before dinner some were prostrate on the decks, and others hastily going to the gunwales casting up accounts—very different however, in their nature and effect, from those of dollars and cents.

Sea-sickness is truly a mystery. What a medley of inexplicable contraries. Now the voyager is in fine spirits and laughs at others who call for poor "Yorrick", and think he is one of the favored few who are permitted to "throw physic to the dogs". But alas poor "Yorick"! Suddenly his equanimity is disturbed by an adverse motion of the vessel and he is prostrate upon the deck, languid, pale, and disturbed by no word so much as dinner.

The person who is seasick, is neither one thing nor the other. He is neither sick, nor well. He is craving food and yet loathing it at the same time. Therefore the unhappy victims condition may be defined as an "unsatisfiable betweenity"!

Contrary to my anticipations, I remained unaffected by the motion of the steamer, which may be attributed to the fact that I rather liked the motion otherwise.

Seven o'clock P.M. – We are yet out-sight of land. The sea continues rough. The white caps or spray flying high up around us, caused by the long swells striking against each other at short intervals. But my head is dizzy, my hand trembles, so I will close only remarking that at noon today the steamer had made in the preceding nautical day – 285 miles. We are therefore 798 miles from our port of departure.

Chapter 34
A Night of Comfortable Repose

October 20th, 1854

The ocean is yet rough, but its violence spent. No land in sight yet. No objects but sky and water are visible. The surface is dark and rough. The white caps are thickly scattered over it and the long swells are annoying to those affected with seasickness, because they cannot recover their equanimity as long as the swells continue. We are still on the Gulf Stream, but will have past them by this evening.

Eight o'clock P.M. – We are once again in sight of land towards the northeast but at a long distance. The long swells are greatly reduced. The white caps are no more seen and the steamer rides smoothly and ... over them. Our seasickness is passing away and we may anticipate a night of comfortable repose.

Chapter 35
In Mind of a Drove of Hogs

October 21ˢᵗ, 1854

The dark clouds have again disappeared. The sky and water have put on their silvery brightness and the surface of the ocean is smooth. All faces around me are smiling and cheerful in the prospect of a fair and cool day but cool days will hardly be among the possible blessings to be enjoyed on this side of the equator. In these latitudes the days and nights are not warm but hot. The breezes are warm, but still they are pro-motive to our comfort. The motion is an agreeable change in the usually inactive state of the air on the ocean as well as on land.

All the cases of seasickness have passed away, but one —a middle-aged person and next bunk neighbor to me. I urged him to get up on his feet and walk about and offered to assist him up on deck, but he declared he cannot raise his head. After several ineffectual attempts to get him up, I found that he was perfectly helpless and had to leave him lay.

Some of the men are constantly on the look out for whales but none of the "Sea Monsters" have as yet made their appearance to give us a view of their "whale ships". We saw several lots of porpoises rolling and tumbling through the water which put me in mind of a drove of hogs.

The steamer's approach stimulated them into wonderful activity, making them jump out of the water, often eight to ten feet high, and fall dashing into the water and throw up columns of spray which may be seen for three or four miles. There are numerous other kinds of fish. We encountered full grown fish twelve or fifteen feet long, lounging in the sea.

The steamers reckoning at noon today had made 579 miles the preceding two days. Thus bringing us 1377 miles from San Francisco.

Chapter 36
Of Long Faces and Stomach 'Squalms'

October 22nd, 1854

The sleep of the laboring man is sweet and so was mine during the last night. Refreshed and thankful, I left my cot at five this morning. The weather was clear and the ocean calm. Soon after sunrise a strong headwind came up, which increased steadily until about six P.M. when it turned into a violent gale.

The waves ran high and the steamer commenced to rock like a cradle, which in a short time brought on a revised and improved edition of the comical scenes enacted a few days ago – of long faces and stomach squalms. Many had recourse to the gunwales of the boat, and make a "bow" to the angry waves.

It is almost impossible to walk the decks in such a sea without the assistance of some object to guard yourself from toppling over and many are creeping along the decks on their hands and feet. We are in sight of land at a distance of eight or ten miles. The steamer makes good headway through the rolling waves which are right in her bow. When striking a wave, she rises gradually on the waves with her bow pointed towards the sky, till she reaches the middle of the wave, when she swings off and sinks down into the deep trough of the sea.

A better idea of this motion may be had by laying a rail or pole across a fence, like school boys are want to do, one sitting on each end of the pole and swinging up and down. The only difference is generally not more than twelve or fifteen feet long, whereas our boat three hundred and twenty-five feet long, which gives it a much longer sweep.

Nine o'clock P.M. – The wind has considerably subsided and the sailors are "ho-ho"ing at the ropes to give all the ship's canvas to the breeze. A ship is a busy place. Even in calm no one is idle. The steamer for the last twenty four hours has made 291 miles. Thus bringing us 1668 miles nearer our home.

Chapter 37
Not One Dime Escaped Them

October 23rd, 1854

I arose from my coverless cot at five this morning and found the sky cloudy and just enough breeze blowing from the shore to make it comfortable. The sea has again resumed its Pacific smoothness. Every person around me wears a pleasant and smiling face, except my old friend who is still confined to his cot of sea sickness.

Nine o'clock A.M. – We arrived in the Bay of Acapulco, an important port of Mexico. The steamer takes in coal here and will be detained here nearly a day. Very few of the passengers take advantage to go ashore as the town is reported to be under blockade by order of Santa Anna. The steamer is anchored about a mile from shore and right in front of the town.

The steam ship company have their coal in boats lying in the bar from whence our steamer gets her supply. The hills and mountains which surround the city, clad in their garniture of perpetual Spring, are an agreeable relief to the monotony of the ocean scenes. The beautiful coconut, lemon and orange groves, which line many parts of the shore and stretch far up the mountain sides, can plainly be seen from our position on the bay.

Shortly after the entrance of the steamer into the bay, a whole navy of the dark skinned men, boys and even some girls, came over from the city to our ship. Some were in canoes or skiffs and others swimming. Some of those in boats had lemons and oranges and other tropical fruit which they offered for sale but the captain of our steamer would not allow them to come on board and forbid the passengers to purchase any fruit on account of being unhealthy but much of it was smuggled on board.

About a half dozen or so of the boys were floating skillfully around the steamer crying "dime, dime throw dime". They would dive down far below the surface of the waters of the bay as often as their wish was gratified by the fun-loving passengers.

At least four or five dollars was thrown overboard and not one dime escaped them. Sometimes, in order to try their skill, the passengers would take a dime and throw it far beyond them. Three or four would go after it and when within sight or ten feet of the spot where it entered the water, they would take a cutoff and dive right down through the water towards it.

After several minutes they would rise to the surface and one of them was sure to have it. These fellows can swim and dive like ducks. Finally all the swimmers left but one who was still floating around on the water, smiling and disclosing a mouth of pearly teeth, and throwing the white of his eyes up at us begging for more dimes.

One of the passengers said, "I am going to give that fellow another chase." He took a silver half dollar, held it up between his thumb and finger to show the fellow what it was. He threw it edgewise into the water at least twenty yards beyond him. He went after it and long before he got to where the money fell, he dived and after a long while, "longer than I would like to be under water", he came up victoriously showing the money. This was a feat almost incredulous, but to those who actually saw it performed.

The coal is conveyed on board the steamer in lighters by the labor of natives who are perfectly naked except from their hips, around which they have tied some fabric which reaches about to the knees.

Huge gold fish, and other fish equally large and of a silvery whiteness, are sluggishly swimming in great numbers near the surface and catching fragments of fruit and other food which is thrown upon the water to attract them.

Five o'clock P.M. – The cannon has just summoned the truant passengers from shore if there was any out. The steamer having "coaled up" and taken in a fresh supply of water, she has turned her dark bows again towards the "deep blue sea". The sky is still overcast with clouds and a stiff breeze blowing from the northeast.

Chapter 38
Broad Sheets of Shining Silver

October 24th, 1854

The clouds of yesterday have all disappeared and the sky is bright and clear with the sun pressing down rather heavily upon us. The wind has changed about and is blowing strong from the southwest, which has again disturbed the smooth surface of the ocean and gives the steamer just a little rolling motion.

But under sails and a heavy pressure of steam, she is gliding swiftly and gracefully through the waves. They are thus crowding steam and sail on in order to make up the time lost for "coaling" yesterday.

Today we passed a flock of flying fish. They are about ten inches long and its head resembles in figure the frogs. Its back is dark brown and the remainder of the body is white. Its wings unite with its sides a little back of the gills and are nearly as long as the body and in shape very nearly resemble those of a bat. They rise out of the water and fly from twenty to fifty feet, keeping about two feet above the surface of the water.

Two o'clock P.M. – A sail in sight at a great distance. She is a brig standing to the southwest. Her studding sail set. Her hull is not distinguishable from the dark elements upon which she rests but her canvas standing beautifully relieved against the sky and lighted by the rays of the sun, look like broad sheets of shining silver spread put upon our view. The steamer at noon today had made the preceding two days including our stoppage, 507 miles thus bringing us 3175 miles from San Francisco.

Chapter 39
A Clever Blow

October 25th, 1854 (Noon)

The heat today is very oppressive and the breezes are not cool and refreshing but warm and therefore impart no invigorating influence. We have crossed the sun's track, which is now north of us, which will be more and more apparent as we sail further south and near the equator.

We are again out of sight of land and no objects in view, but the blazing sun and sky overhead and the water and fishes underneath.

Eight o'clock P.M. – The scene this evening has suddenly changed. The sky just now so bright and clear, is in a surprisingly short time, overcast with dark and threatening clouds. Soon the rain came pouring down in torrents. The wind roared through the rigging of the steamer. The thunder rolled and the forked lightning held a perfect revelry in the heavens.

The waves began to rise higher and higher and beat with fearful violence against the steamer, which careens deeply, rolls and rocks, and now her bow looks upward toward the threatening clouds, then she sinks fearfully down into the depths of the sea.

Every officer and sailor is at his post. The Captain's glance is rapid, and his step frequent and hurried, in issuing orders, but betrays no fear. Not so, however, with us "land lubbers", as may be confessed, that all the previously acquired feelings of security vanish in a moment, and vividly realizing our true situation. Perhaps many hundred miles from the nearest land, no other sail in sight, surrounded with almost total darkness, confined to a structure, though strong and sound, yet only the workmanship of man. In a storm of wind and rain with the waves of the limitless waters beating fearfully and heavily against her massive timbers.

These reflections were deeply impressed upon our minds with the truth of the frailty and littleness of the mightiest human agency. The captain keeping the passengers in fearful suspense for sometime, he gazed up into the darkened clouds, and turning himself to the assembled passengers, very coolly said, "A clever blow, but it's about over." We then took a long breath and retired to our bunks thinking of those sweet lines – "home, home, there's no place like home."

Chapter 40
A Glorious Light Upon the Surrounding Scene

October 26ʰ, 1854

The storm of last night has disappeared and the ocean has again resumed its pacific smoothness. The sun in the firmament has risen bright and beautiful upon the darkness that so lately rested upon us.

Today we have decided evidence of the near approach to the equator. The shadows we cast at noon today are very short. Passengers upon the quarter deck are huddled together under the awnings and those not admitted to this privilege are seeking protection from the burning heat in the covered passageways on the lower deck. Many a wish is sent forth for one of the many cool, cool breezes that are uselessly wandering about in the north. But another day is gone, and with it the hot sun has disappeared in the western sky and night is again folding her mantle around us. The moon and stars are appearing in the canopy of heaven and omit a glorious light upon the surrounding scene. Scarcely a breeze is ruffling the smooth surface of this broad blue ocean. The steamer at noon today has made 555 miles for the last two days, thus bringing us 2730 miles nearer our homes.

Chapter 41
As Though a Light was Shining upon Them

October 27, 1854

Last night was one of uncommon beauty. The moon and stars, in the forefront of the evening, were very bright. No wind, and the surface of the ocean was smooth and shone like a limitless mirror. But shortly after ten o'clock, the sky became overcast with clouds and everything around us was shrouded in darkness.

Being seated among a number of others upon the quarter deck, and resting my elbow on the gunwales, looking into the water, I observed that the ruffles of waves thrown out by the motion of the steamer appeared as though a light was shining upon them and looking down alongside of the steamer to see where the light came from, I ascertained that no light was emitted from that source.

Calling the attention of others to this strange light, we perceived numerous streaks and flashes of a whitish light all around the steamer and on a closer observation, we ascertained that they were caused by the motion of innumerable fishes both large and small, darting away in every direction on the approach of the steamer.

Now and then a large fish would shoot away, leaving a track behind him, which could be seen for a moment, at a distance of several rods. Some more slow than others, could be plainly seen, their length, shape and even their fins.

We were informed by an old tar that this phosphorescent light was caused by the water being more salty and stronger than other places. I stayed on deck until midnight, looking at this phenomenon which however had nearly disappeared by this time.

I arose at six this morning, went on deck, found the weather fine, the sky bright and clear, a sail in sight but a great distance from us. Land also the first sight that we saw since we left Acapulco, but on nearer approach it turns out to be only an island, which from a distance had the appearance of a snow bank piled against the sky and glistening in the morning sun, which is caused by the reflection of the rays of light. A nearer approach, however, dispels the illusion and shows us the dark summits of the island.

This has been an unusually hot, close and sultry day. The steamer has not kept her "speed good". The last twenty-four hours on account of being among shoals and soundings, have only made 261 miles. We were therefore at noon today 2991 miles from the port of San Francisco and only about twenty-four hours sail from Panama.

Chapter 42
Me Carry Your Bag!

October 28, 1854

Today the steamer's bow was turned northward towards the Bay of Panama. The weather in the morning was cloudy and a little rain, but shortly after sunrise, the clouds disappeared and the day was again hot, close and sultry. But this did not prevent the passengers from keeping a sharp lookout for the first indication of the main land.

About nine o'clock A.M. the welcome sound of "Land, Land!" was announced by one of the passengers, when everyone raised their hand over their eyes. Eyes strained in the direction indicated, but nothing could be seen, except a little dark spot about the size of a hat, appearing to rest upon the surface of the ocean.

This spot, however, increased as we advanced and in a very short time it was discovered to be the dusky outline of a lofty mountain, called by the sailors "Mount Darien", situated in the interior of the isthmus.

We passed many islands during the day, some of which were piles of naked moss-grown rocks, and others were studded with trees and shrubbery. About noon, land appeared towards the northwest rising just above the surface of the sea.

As we advanced, the elevation of the shore increased and gently rising hills appeared in the interior. The passengers during the afternoon were engaged in arranging their luggage, and preparing to leave the steamer, as it was announced that we would reach Panama by evening.

At half-past five P.M. a faint blue outline of the old city of Panama can be seen right ahead over the steamer's bow. But at a considerable distance, and appears to rise directly out of the sea. The island of Taboga is also in sight, which is occupied by the Pacific Mail Steamship Company as a depot, being at a considerable distance from the mainland, its climate is salubrious and delightful. Invalids resort here to await the arrival of steamers from San Francisco.

Nine o'clock P.M. – The cannons boom announced the arrival of the steamer which is now riding at anchor in the bay about three miles from town, as it cannot approach nearer on account of rocks and shoals.

These old Spanish ports seldom have docks and passengers and luggage are conveyed to the shore in canoes or "bungos", rowed by dark-skinned and darker-minded natives of the country.

The Steamer has made the last thirty-six hours, three hundred and four miles, thus making the distance from here to San Francisco by the steamer's track, three thousand two hundred and ninety-five miles (3295). This ends the first division of my long journey and the scenes will be greatly changed.

In the course of about half an hour after the ponderous wheels of the steamer had stopped, the steamer was surrounded by twenty-five or thirty canoes or bungos rowed by dusky natives. All was bustle and anxiety among the passengers and the noise and confusion now became general. Each passenger was anxious to go on shore first and rushed down the narrow stairway erected for that purpose and crowding on the canoes and loading them down to the waters edge.

In the meantime the natives were fighting among themselves. Those that had loaded could not get out, on account of others trying to force their way in, pushing the boats of one another around, cursing and swearing and striking one another over their woolly heads with oars hard enough to fell an ox and putting the life of those on board in jeopardy.

The noise and confusion was ebbing high for about three quarters of an hour, which time was consumed in loading and departing. In the course of about an hour they came back again for another load, when again the same scene ensued as before.

My companion, I and two or three others, concluded to stand aloof and wait till the rush had somewhat subsided, which lasted till near midnight. After the third trip was made, the rush was over and six of us took seats in a bungo rowed by two natives who landed us with ten or twelve feet of the shore in shallow water of six inches deep.

Here we were surrounded by at least fifty of the dusky rascals who demanded to carry us and our baggage on shore for two bits or twenty cents. Two or three took hold of me, saying "me carry you", and another one, "me carry your bag", at the same time grabbing at it. I disengaged myself of those having a hold of me and jerking my bag out of the others hand telling them that I can go on shore myself.

I got up on the bow of the boat, told my companions to come on, and made a leap to pass over the heads of those who were in the way but before I came down into the water, two of the black rascals caught me and landed me safely on shore for which privilege they demanded each two "bits".

My companions were served in like manner and in order to make the best out of a bad bargain, we forked over and left in double quick as we were about the last who came on shore and did not consider ourselves very safe among our black companions especially at this hour, midnight.

We hurried uptown through dark, narrow and filthy streets to the American Hotel, but this and several other houses that we came to were crowded. Finally we were recommended to a restaurant kept by an American some distance up town.

Still being accosted on every hand by some of the dusky natives who offered their services in any capacity, we engaged one to guide us to the place indicated. We traveled several dark streets or alleys, till we reached the place. Here we found a number of our ship companions who came here in advance of us.

We ordered supper to which we have done ample justice as we had nothing since breakfast. Lodging we were also accommodated with, minus bed clothing. Some slept on the bare floor, others had bunks to sleep upon, for which commodity we paid one dollar and supper the same.

But it may safely be asserted that no one hurt himself by sleeping too much on this occasion. My fellow travelers all went to roost, so I will close my journal and follow suit.

Chapter 43
A Perfect Mania

October 29, 1854
Panama City, Panama

This morning the whole house was in an uproar long before daylight appeared in the eastern sky, or I might say rather it was not quiet all night. I got up at five, no, I should say, I came down, as I occupied the fifth tier of bunks, one above the other, in rather close proximity to the rafters.

I clambered down from one bunk to another, like coming down a huge ladder. I went down stairs and out in the open air, as the position which I have occupied in the upper regions was rather close. The sky was clear but the atmosphere was very oppressive.

Being anxious to make the transit from here to the southern terminus of the railroad as soon as could conveniently be done, which was distant seventeen miles and had to be accomplished on the backs of mules or donkeys kept for that purpose by "Joy & Co.", who were employed by the Pacific Steam Ship Company to transfer the mail, gold, and express matter to Aspinwall.

Our breakfast being hurried up, which when ready was soon dispatched. After which we went down town to the office of "Joy & Co.", to get our mule checks, as we or nearly all had through tickets, and were therefore entitled to a mule each.

Arriving at the office we found that nearly all the passengers were there already and anxious to get their checks in order to have the first choice at the mules which were kept in a large enclosure close by, in charge of a number of natives who saddled them and delivered them over to those who presented their checks, as fast as they came in.

This company owns at least twelve or fifteen hundred mules for transportation of passengers, mails, gold, etc.

Wagons are not used in this country. A report was current since early morning that half the mules were on the other side awaiting the transit passengers from New York, which leaves but a limited supply for the emigration on this side, which is the principle cause for the great rush at the office.

Finally, however, after much crowding and pushing, and swearing, the tickets were all exchanged for checks. But long before this was accomplished it was reported that all the mules were gone and at least three hundred of us were as yet unprovided with one.

There were private parties, native, who owned mules to hire but they wanted ten dollars besides our checks for a mule which we considered an exorbitant price and would not pay it. Some few who were anxious to get out of this place, paid the difference and left, but the greater portion of us would not accede to this demand as we were entitled to a mule or an equivalent to our checks which were counted worth ten dollars.

Therefore another rush was made to the office for satisfaction, but on arriving there the office was closed. This caused considerable excitement among the disappointed crowd and a great deal of swearing in the bargain. After a short consultation, it was agreed that a party would go in quest of the officers, who after considerable delay, brought them back.

The office was reopened and the checks were handed in, which were stamped and referred to the office of the Mail Steamship Company which was located in the lower portion of the town, near where we landed on the previous night. To this place we went in double quick, presented our checks and received the cash for them, ten dollars.

We felt quite elated with the ten dollars in our pockets. We could save them by taking it on foot. On our return to the square or plaza, there were still a number of natives who had mules to hire but they wanted sixteen dollars for one.

We told them they might "go to grass with their jackasses. We would rather walk before paying one dollar per mile." They said, "You can no walk. You go in mud over your knees."

We told them, "We'll risk the mud." Four or five of us being together, having nothing to carry but our carpet bags, we concluded to risk the latter mode of transit. Arriving at the boarding house, we made preparations, after a short rest, to leave.

In the meantime I will give a hasty description of this old town which appears as though it might have been constructed before "Noah's" time. A person might safely challenge the world to produce another place, more dirty, dingy and dilapidated than Panama. The streets are narrow and paved with rough stone, which have been worn without repairs for ages.

They are lowest in the middle and all the refuse from the dwellings are thrown into them. The buildings generally are constructed of brick or stone and are plastered and painted a color which once was white. They are from two to six stories in height. The ground rooms of the houses, occupied by the black natives and the Spanish, are used as stables and in many instances the occupant and his family are boon companions with the Mules.

The founding of this city is attributed to Fernando Cortez more than three hundred years ago. He raised a wall of rock and earth around this old town, a portion of which still remains, and it is curious to observe that the cement used in its construction is more durable than rock. The latter is worn away by the action of time, leaving the former protruding far beyond it.

The old cathedral still stands, venerable and gloomy in its dilapidation and decay, and is romantic for the mysterious connection with the cruel annals of the shadowy past. Its dome is covered with shells of the pearl oyster, which reflects the rays of the sun and glisten in his beams as brightly now as they did two hundred years ago.

The ruins of the old Jesuit College and several monasteries, covering a large extant and overgrown with ivy, are interesting and prominent objects for examination. Many thousands have been educated within those crumbling walls and have worshiped therein, and passed away generations ago.

This town, especially the modern portion, is very regularly laid out. The streets intersect at right angles. A few of the dwellings are enclosed by high walls and the coconut trees, vines and other foliage, rising above and blending over them, relieve the dry and gloomy exterior and are suggestive of the fragrance and comfort which reign within the enclosure.

The population of the city is estimated at six thousand. The number of Americans and Europeans does not exceed three hundred. The inhabitants are principally Negroes and Indians, but the intermarriages with Europeans, Spaniards, a mixed race has been produced which inherits a few of the good and many of the bad qualities of both original stocks. Ignorance, treachery, dishonesty, cowardice and indolence are universal characteristics and the devotion for gambling amounts to a perfect mania.

As in other tropical countries, the year here has but two seasons. The dry season being between December and June, the remainder of the year being the wet season. The climate is very unhealthy for foreigners, especially those from the North.

The temperature for many weeks in the dry season is stationary at 95 degrees and even 100 degrees. Bilious fevers and dysentery are the most prevailing diseases.

Several kinds of tropical fruits are abundant and cheap. Oranges, figs, plantains, olives, egg plant, coconut, bananas, grapes, etc. are exposed for sale on the corners of the streets.

About eight o'clock all the bells of the city commenced to chime which made a considerable noise. Very soon the inhabitants were seen wending their way, in great numbers, to the several churches and habited in various costumes. The men generally are clad in white linen from head to foot, with a broad rim panama hat and the women were done up in light linen gowns with immense frills about their necks with nearly the entire shoulders and breasts bare with a broad rim panama on their heads.

The whiteness of their dresses was in sharp contrast with their tawny skins. I also noticed several priests, attired in long black gowns, small clothes, white stockings, pumps and three-cornered hats.

Nine o'clock A.M. we shouldered our bags and followed after the long procession of pack mules and riders who have just left and are passing through the Gorgona Gate. This passage is a lofty archway of stone, opening through the old walls of the city which is surmounted with a cross and a ball. On the outside of the gate the whole cavalcade of pack mules stopped.

There were at least seventy five mules in the train, packed with gold, mails and express matter besides the small navy of native infantry who are hired by the company to guard against robbery on the way, including all the passengers both riders and footmen, presenting quite a novel and interesting appearance as it was moving along single file.

Judging by the awkward appearance of the mules, they are by no means very elegant, nor obliging or comfortable conveyances for freshmen, especially on the Isthmus. Several of the ladies were clad in masculine nether garments and assumed the position of the sterner sex on the backs of the mules.

The greater portion of the road over which we are traveling was constructed by Cortez to expedite the passage of troops and ammunition of war, from the Atlantic to the Pacific. This road, as I am informed, was constructed at least two hundred and thirty years ago and has the appearance as if it had not been improved or repaired from that period to the present time. It was originally a paved way, the stone was set edge-wise and was about four or five feet in width and was intended only for footmen and mules. As I stated before, wheel carriages are not in use in this country.

The first three or four miles out of the city, being over level and comparatively tolerable road, but the remainder as far as Gorgona, which was the place of our destination, can never be so graphically described as to convey a correct idea of the real condition. The person who travels over it in the "wet season" will never be able to forget the adventure. I am confident that I shall never forget mine to the longest days of my existence. Not because I ventured out on foot. I have seen those on mule back who fared considerably worse than those on foot. In some places the paving has been pressed so far below the surface that the way was a perfect canal, filled with mud and water to the depth of one and even two feet, in the bottom of which are loose stones.

Over these the little mule or donkey stumbles and often falls, bringing its rider to the bottom and covering him with mud and water from head to foot. At other places where the soil is more firm, the paving is loose and much displaced, although the mud is not very deep, the rider is liable to be precipitated upon the stones at the hazard of bruised flesh and broken bones.

In some parts the road appears to have been either worn down by water or by the feet of mules to a depth of from two to thirty feet and at the bottom it is not more than one or two feet wide, increasing gradually towards the top of the gorge to six or eight feet.

Several of these passes with but short intervals, are a mile in length and the mud and water in them are from one to two feet deep. The traveler in these passes is not without danger, as it will occasionally happen that a train of pack mules, will be met here when the unlucky traveler has no alternative, he must turn his mule in the narrow passage and retrace his steps to the nearest turnout or the pack mule with its burden of trunks, bags or boxes, will go "pell-mell" over donkey and rider, for in such a dilemma it knows no duty but to "go ahead" and the greater obstacle the more ungovernable and resolute he becomes.

In such encounters, valuable property is often damaged or destroyed and many accidents occur to the traveler. It requires no Yankee to guess what becomes of some of the mail bags, if he takes but one trip across the Isthmus. I saw several mules loaded with mail matter, which trampled over and emptied their contents into the mud and tread upon it, which those who are in charge, if not convenient, are not very particular about picking them up and reloading them again.

If we take into account the impediments, difficulties, and dangers to be experienced on such a road, we add the temperature of the climate at perhaps 90 or 95 degrees and frequent copious tropical rains, with some well grounded apprehensions of robbery and murder, the whole will give one a faint description of the transit of the Isthmus at Panama.

Mules often fall on the way and the rider is obliged to proceed on foot. Amongst others, I saw a lady whose beast

161

had fallen and was abandoned for the safer progress of the pedestrian. She was literally covered with mud. Her hair was hanging down over her shoulders, her dress had been torn from her knees down, and with her dripping bonnet in hand, she was resolutely making her way in the company of some men, who like ourselves had chosen to cross the Isthmus on foot.

But some generous-hearted fellow overtaking her on the way, had compassion upon her pitiful state and offered his mule, which after some persuasion she accepted the kind offer, while he was jogging along, through the mud on foot.

Along the road were several houses or shanties built of cane and thatched with palm or plantain, at which travelers could rest and also obtain poor refreshments. My companion, I and several others, stopped at one of these establishments shortly after noon, to rest and refresh ourselves, the sun being broiling hot, there was not a dry thread on me. It is reported that in the time of the wet season, it rains every day. I remarked to my companions that I would like to see a big shower of rain, as it might have a tendency to cool off a little.

A native standing by and hearing the remark said, "You get much rain before night. More than you like."

While stopping here, two sick persons were carried by who were reclining upon hammocks, suspended from long poles and a powerful native at each end with a long staff each in his hand, to guide themselves by through mud and water. These persons were not able to ride on mule back, consequently they had to be carried by these natives.

About two P.M. we heard the distant rumbling of thunder. I told companions that perhaps the natives predictions will come to pass, which was truly verified in less than half an hour from the first intimation that we had of thunder.

The sky was overcast with black clouds, the thunder rolled over our heads with a fearful noise and vibrated through every nook and corner. The lightning held a perfect revelry in the clouds and among dense jungle around us and almost simultaneously the rain came pouring down in torrents.

This was a regular tropical thunder shower, and such thundering and lightning, I never experienced in my life. It continued for one hour and a half without intercession. We took shelter in one of the shanties along the road, not exactly to keep from getting wet, as we were already as wet as could be, but to be out of the weather which was fearful and almost blinding. We stopped in for about half an hour or so but fearing that night would overtake us before reaching our destination, as we had yet five or six miles to go, we started out again and faced the rain, thunder and lightning and waded through mud and water up to our knees. This was unavoidable. We could neither turn to the left nor the right on account of the density of this tropical jungle, so we had to follow in the footsteps of the mules.

We made out to reach the terminus of the railroad just at night fall, muddy, wet, and weary, and barefooted and my feet all cut up by sharp stones. I had but a light pair of shoes. They were soon cut up and finally I left them sticking in the mud.

I would have willingly paid out my ten dollars mule money for a pair of boots if they could be had on the way but there was none so I had to do the best I could under the circumstances.

On arriving at the depot, I divested myself of part of my soiled garments, and made them an offering to the Shade of Fernando Cortez, the immortal author of this indescribable road.

The New York passengers about five hundred, had also just come in on the cars from Aspinwall. The little town is crowded to repletion. No less than fourteen hundred passengers are here, both men, women, and children and only two hotels and a few cane huts and shanties scattered about among the coconut trees. The population principally natives and Indians, is about two hundred. The locality is low, wet and very unhealthy.

Every foot of shelter was taken up, both the hotels and shanties, and even some cars standing a considerable distance down the road were crowded.

I was fortunate enough to procure a cot in a large sleeping apartment upstairs in one of the hotels, in which there were no less than seventy-five weary wanderers scattered promiscuously, men, women, and children, over the floor and in bunks and many were swinging in suspended hammocks and as many as could find a recumbent position, took it cool on the wet floor.

I retired to my cot supper-less, because the "Mine Hosts" larder ran short of provision, which was rather slow in being replenished. Consequently many like myself went to their pillow-less cots without their suppers.

But there was very little rest and much less sleep on this night because we were assailed by mosquitoes from above and fleas from below. Some rolled and tumbled in their cots. Some slapped and scratched and still others kicked and scolded and some were laughing and talking.

Some time during the night a woman or mother started up and called "Billy! Billy! Where are you?" – no answer from Billy. Away goes the enquirer wading through the recumbent multitude an crawling under the bunks and suspended sleepers, till Billy is found and taken to the maternal embrace.

"O dear!" cries one, "I shall surely melt!"

"Hope you may!" growls a crusty old fellow, "Then ye'll be quiet!"

"Ha, ha, ha", from a good-humored fellow away up in a corner. "No melting here tonight. Can't stand that." Scratch, scratch, in this cot. Slap, slap, slap, in another.

"Well", exclaims a female voice, "I believe this is the mosquito country, sure enough."

"All mosquito!" responds another.

"Rightly named", cries a third.

And so the scene progresses until daylight brought relief to the weary and the restless.

Chapter 44
A Man's Life for Nearly Every Sleeper

October 30, 1854

Another night is passed and such a night. I paid "Mine Host" one dollar for my coverless cot and sallied forth in quest of both for something to eat and to purchase a pair of shoes, if such as article can be found in this tropical country.

I searched the whole town and was about giving it up for a bad job, when I espied a little shop among the coconut trees. Here, fortunately, was one pair on sale which were a few sizes too large, but I purchased them for four dollars. At the same place I also obtained a tolerable good breakfast which consisted principally of tropical fruits done up in various styles and some coffee without sugar or milk.

There were numerous other travelers eating here. The place was kept by an old native and his woman, who were both quite friendly and talkative. I paid one dollar for my breakfast, after which I went in quest of my companion whom I have not seen since the night before. I soon found him among a large crowd waiting for their breakfast at one of the hotels.

I told him he could probably get breakfast where I had mine so I returned with him to the place and told the old native that I had another hungry person here who would like to have something to eat if he could accommodate him. He said "Oh yes, I guess we can find something for him yet."

After breakfast we repaired to the depot, but on reaching the place we learned that no train would leave before eleven o'clock A.M. In the mean time the New York passengers are making ready and leaving this place for Panama. They will have to go over the same route that we have come and many perhaps will share the fate that was meted out to many of us—of mules getting mired in the mud and water

166

and perhaps a good tropical thunder shower to keep them cool.

But they have one advantage over us, which is the selection of mules as they are all on this side of the transit. They have therefore a better choice to select of the best and strongest.

Shortly before eleven o'clock, the welcome sound of the whistle announced the approach of the railway train from Aspinwall, which was coming in backwards and stopped before the company's office. Here the gold, express matter, and piles of mail bags were stored into cars while the dense crowd of passengers, panting, were pushing and scrambling to get on the train.

At precisely eleven o'clock A.M. the locomotive shrieked and the long train moved out of the dusky old town, following endless curves and slowly winding around foot hills and through dense jungles, on our way to the Atlantic, distant forty miles.

Along the road are many dwellings and some villages with steep-roofed cabins, huts, and shanties, thatched with tiles, grass, or cane, with walls of sticks, and plaster. They look dry and cool, but during the wet season they must admit water like sieves. These hovels are principally occupied by natives who are constantly employed to repair the road and keep it from being washed away by rains or crumbled or covered by the irrepressible vegetation.

Here prolific nature has produced the richest, densest, vegetation in the world. An impenetrable tangle of mangoes, plantains, palms, bananas, limes, Indian rubber trees, and thousands of shrubs and parasites new to Northern eyes.

The whole Isthmus without exception is a vast jungle of trees and cane brakes, gay with gorgeous flowers and various kinds of birds with brilliant plumage. Monkeys and parrots chatter on the branches of trees. Wild beasts hide in the dingles. Insects swarm in the swamps, huge reptiles crawl along the cozy soil, darkened by thick foliage which shuts out the light of the rich tropical heavens.

The railway of the Isthmus was begun in 1848 which was a truly great undertaking but the greatest wonder of all, to me, is how a party of surveyors could ever penetrate through this wild, dense and impenetrable jungle. The road

*is now finished within twelve or fourteen miles of Panama
and the cost per mile is said to be about one hundred and
sixty thousand dollars. The work has again and again been
suspended for the fever breeding air poisoned all who
breathed it.*

*Natives, West Indies, Irish, French, Germans, Austrians,
Coolies, and Chinese, were successively employed as
laborers, but to all it proved fatal. The forty miles now
completed are ridged with graves and it is said to have cost
a man's life for nearly every sleeper on the road. I was
informed by a person who assured us that, out of two
thousand Coolies brought over from China two years ago,
all have died but fifteen.*

*Jamaica Negroes, and whites from our Northern States,
are better proof against the climate and are now employed
to finish the work. On our way towards Aspinwall, we
followed down the Chagres River for several miles, against
whose muddy current, natives used to paddle early
California emigrants up in canoes.*

*At that time it required from six to eight days to make a
trip from the Atlantic to the Pacific and but half that time for
the return trip being downstream and made better
headway.*

*At five o'clock P.M. we arrived at Apsinwall, sometimes
called Navy Bay. This is a new port established by the
steam ship company, at a place about six miles east from
the old town Chagres. The company at this port have a large
and commodious office and an extensive dock and depot
which enables first class steamers to come to the wharf
without ferriage.*

*The town contains but one principle street, besides the
small portion of a town which is built on a narrow strip of
land running out into the bay across which a foot bridge of
plank is built above high water mark, which enables
pedestrians to cross over and repass from one portion of the
town to the other.*

*The buildings are of wood, one and two stories in height
and are painted white. Several of them used as hotels, are
large and imposing structures. The inhabitants are chiefly
natives, Jamaica Negroes and Americans and contains a
population of less than six hundred. The locality of the town*

is low, marshy and contains arable land. The place is chiefly sustained by the operations of the company and will probably never be a place of great importance.

Having taken up my quarters in company with many others, in one of the hotels, where I hope to enjoy a comfortable nights rest after a two days transit of the Isthmus, during which time I enjoyed but little rest and much less sleep. I will therefore close my journal for the present and await the events of another day.

Aspinwall City from the Lighthouse (modern Colon, Panama)

Chapter 45
Many a Wistful Eye was Cast Seaward

October 31, 1854

I left my quarters at a late hour this morning having enjoyed a tolerable degree of repose. I feel considerably refreshed from the fatigues of the past two days. The sky overhead is bright and clear but the atmosphere is still very oppressive. Breakfast was soon announced and about a hundred made a stampede for the dining room in which were arranged two large tables around which were seated one hundred and ten persons by my own count.

The table contained but an indifferent supply of eatables, consisting principally of salted meats, fresh fish from the bay, stale bread, sea-biscuit, tea and coffee without milk or cream and a poor article of imported butter which when set before us was but a single remove from grease.

Culinary vegetables are not raised in this part of the country, having appeased the cravings of the inner man, as well as could be expected under the circumstances, for which we paid one dollar, or three dollars for supper, lodging and breakfast, each separately in advance.

We now sallied forth to the company's office, to ascertain the precise time for the departure of our steamer for New York, which was now lying at the wharf. But on inquiry we were informed that it would not leave until the following day at eleven o'clock. This was rather bad news for us, since we all wished to get out of this as soon as possible.

This delay was occasioned by the non-arrival of the steamer from New Orleans, which was due, but in case it does not make its appearance, by the allotted time tomorrow, all the passengers who have tickets for New Orleans, will have to proceed in the North Star, which is the name of the steamer for New York, as far as the island of

Cuba, at which place they will be landed to await transportation thence to New Orleans.

There were about three hundred passengers, among whom was my companion, who had tickets for New Orleans. Many a wistful eye was cast seaward during the day, for the glimpse of the expected steamer, but without avail. The day passed regardless of our anxieties, so we had to spend another night in this dreary, wretched and desolate place, which is a perfect imposition upon travelers from one end of the town to the other, paying exorbitant prices for all that we get and for many things that we do not get, or in other words paying high prices for inferior articles.

But another day is past and night is again closing her dark mantle around us and with it I will close my journal and try to find repose in dream land.

Chapter 46
Her Appointed Course Homeward

Steamer North Star

November 1, 1854
Aspinwall, Isthmus of Panama

Having enjoyed a comfortable night's rest, I was up bright and early, and after partaking of a poor apology for a breakfast, my companion, I, and nearly all the passengers repaired to the lone wharf beyond the gates of which our steamer was moored.

Here we waited impatiently the time for our departure. From this point we had a fine view of the surrounding bay and of the ocean as far out as eyes could reach. Scarcely a zephyr ruffles the broad expanse of water. Everybody was on the "que-vive" for the first sight of the New Orleans steamer which was now momentarily expected.

At about ten o'clock the welcome sight of a sail hove in sight far out upon the ocean. Her sails just appearing above the surface of the ocean and resting against the sky like a white and shining cloud. All eyes are turned in the direction to greet her welcome coming.

Slowly she rises out of the water. The convexity of the ocean hides the hull of a vessel ten miles away. How beautifully she rides her native element, her sails are all set, her ensign is floating proudly from her masthead.

In the course of half an hour, she was close in sight, and seemed to stand almost entirely out of the water, through which she was gliding like a seabird, her decks crowded with men and women, shouting and waving hats and handkerchiefs. Her flags were lowered and guns fired and she was soon rounding to at her moorings alongside of the wharf.

Directly after discharging her passengers and mails, the boom of our steamer's cannon announced its readiness to receive the passengers. Gold and mails having previously been shipped on board.

My companion and I taking a final leave of each other, I followed after the anxious crowd, through the long narrow gangway which had a gate at each end and one in the middle at each of which we had to present our tickets for inspection which were closely scrutinized one after the other.

As soon as all our passengers were on board, the steamers cannon which had just arrived, also announced its readiness for her passengers who were now coming as fast as they could get through the gates, through which none could pass without a ticket.

This is a necessary precaution, in order to guard against any one smuggling himself on board the ship, which is however, frequently done, regardless of their vigilance, but generally during the night while the steamer is lying to at her moorings. If any are fortunate enough to reach the ship unobserved, they hide themselves in the hold of the steamer until well out at sea, when they come out of their hiding places and will, as a matter of course, be taken along to the first port. In the meantime they are put to hard labor of the most drudgery that is found on shipboard.

At eleven o'clock A.M. the steamer's cannon boomed forth her parting signal. The ponderous wheels are in motion and the noble steamer with her precious freight of human life and gold, swings gracefully from her moorings and glides through the smooth waters of the bay on her appointed course homeward. In a short time, as we recede

173

from the shore, Aspinwall appeared but a dusky speck in the distance.

Now we are out on the ocean and the same scene is commenced on shipboard that I witnessed on the Golden Gate. All is bustle and confusion among the passengers, who are taking possession of their bunks which are without bedding, and making arrangements for comfort during an eight days sail.

Our number of passengers on board are about five hundred and forty and but a comparatively few of whom have cabin tickets. This is owing, I presume, to the fact that cabin passage is three hundred dollars while steerage is but half that price and so far, I must confess, I am perfectly satisfied with the choice I have made. I thought before starting out, that the accommodations must be poor if a person could not outlive them twenty-five or thirty days.

The deck hands, soon after getting under way, were busily engaged in arranging and stowing away luggage and putting the steamer in trim. The order and system of which is the same substantially as that of the steamer Golden Gate. But the North Star is a much smaller steamer and more liable to roll, and less airy—her room capacities not so spacious and comfortable and her ports are very small. There are several sick persons on board but it is hoped that the higher latitudes will soon restore them to health and happiness.

In is not my purpose to describe minutely the things that may transpire on our voyage to New York which will materially be the same as those described on the Pacific, with the exception perhaps, of bright clear skies, calm seas, and gentle breezes.

Old Neptune may rouse up from his six days siesta and leave his coral caves, and come blustering down from the North, to give our tiny craft an angry shake with a sprinkle of the briny spray. I shall therefore only record such incidents worthy of note which may occur on the way.

On the third day after leaving port a death occurred on the ship. One of the sick passengers ended the voyage of life. I could not repress the thought, how sad thus to die, far away from home and friends. No loving lips to whisper words of hope and comfort in the dying ear. Even in seasons of health and prosperity, how dear are all the associations of home, but doubly dear when sickness prostrates us or adversity overtakes us.

"But all seasons are thine, o Death". When the first rays of the morning sun appeared in the eastern sky, the body was brought on deck, appropriately attired for burial. It was securely rolled in canvas, a heavy weight attached to his feet. The cot on which it rested was then brought to the side of the ship. No prayer was offered up. No funeral hymn was sung. Slowly and solemnly the body was raised and at the appointed signal, it was let go and disappeared beneath the swelling waves of the deep, deep, blue sea. One plunge and the sea rolled on. The wind swept over the restless surface, sighing a requiem.

The passengers silently retired from the solemn scene and all was over and soon forgotten by them, many of whom were seated in groups upon the quarter deck, amusing themselves in various games of cards—some reading and others laughing and talking. The sad event apparently produced but a slight impression upon their minds, many feeling perhaps, that it was another's fate and not their own and the subject was banished as one in which they have no concern.

On the morning of the fourth day, we were in sight of Jamaica Island distant about one mile. Many sail boats are in sight. Some of which are near enough to our steamer to exchange salutations with the woolly head in yellow shirts who are superintending their "fishing tackle", located in these waters.

I could distinctly see the inhabitants moving on the shore. The land appeared to be covered with underbrush scattered among which were many towering trees and further inland were also tolerable lofty mountains. Tropical fruits grow here spontaneously and in abundance. The soil however, is not cultivated with much industry or skill and the inhabitants principally are Jamaica Negroes who are characteristically both indolent and ignorant.

Later in the day we stood off the Island of Cuba, distant about forty miles northwest and shall therefore not be favored with a distinct view of her most Catholic Majesty's Jewel. "The Bright Little Isle of the Ocean". We have but a dim outline of some of her lofty mountains which are scarcely distinguishable from the clouds appearing only just above the surface of the ocean.

Since the first night after leaving Aspinwall, we encountered strong headwinds, which have been steadily increasing until on the fifth day of our voyage they turned into a perfect gale through which we experienced the sharp contrast to the smooth Pacific and the shining capacity of our steamer for rolling and pitching.

It was difficult to decide which was the hardest, to keep in our berth through the night, dress in the morning, or eat during the day. Those of the passengers whose berths were crosswise in the vessel would sometimes almost stand on their feet and in a few moments the motion would be reversed and their heads go down in a corresponding manner.

My cot was placed lengthwise and I could with difficulty keep my position without adhering to some firm object. After daylight appeared, we left our cots and were staggering about the boat, grasping at the berth posts or other objects, battling to keep on our feet. We could not go on deck on account of the huge waves drenching the deck with spray. Many of the passengers were prostrate with seasickness. Some of them were shamed to own up and declared that they were merely suffering from headache.

But the sea on such occasions is a relentless leveler without the slightest regard for personal prejudices. I was among the fortunate ones. I did not feel the slightest effects of sea sickness on the whole voyage.

It is a perpetual wonder to landsmen how a steamer can ride such waves, sometimes the wheels are submerged, and a moment after lifted far out of the water. But as long as the waves strike her bows or stern, at a right angle, she breasts them easily, but a single broadside wave would be likely to swamp her.

At short intervals the steamer would make a tremendous lurch rolling or tumbling every loose article about the vessel. After lasting nearly twenty-four hours, the gale abated considerably and we wretched mortals began to creep out of our close quarters and went on deck which we could with difficulty walk without clinging to some safe object.

In looking out upon the angry and disturbed ocean, it is wonderful to see the huge white-capped waves rolling and swaying to and fro, striking against each other and sending the spray high into the air. The pretext for breakfast and dinner was very shallow by many of the passengers but by supper time, everyone felt inclined for something to eat and at the usual hour, we all made our way down in the hull of the vessel in which locality our meals were served instead of between decks as on the steamer Golden Gate.

There are two long tables suspended from the ceiling lengthwise, one on each side of the vessel. The sea still being very rough, and the steamer rolling and pitching and careening considerably to one side, making the floor of the vessel like a tolerable steep roof.

We had just taken our position in the two long rows, one at the upper and at the lower side of the table, to which we were clinging for support and swaying to and fro by the motion of the vessel. Our meal on this occasion consisted of soup which was served in large tin dishes to which with difficulty, we helped ourselves. In a moment the steamer made a tremendous lurch to one side throwing those standing at the upper side against the table which struck those at the lower side with considerable force throwing them back against the side of the vessel and some attempting to save themselves fell over on their backs with soup, dishes, and everything on the table came tumbling after them on the careening floor, dancing a Virginia reel.

The scene presented was truly ridiculous. Some jested and had a good laugh about the incident and others who received rather more than their proportional share of soup looked crestfallen and out of temper. Some few took their portion with true nonchalance.

After crossing the Gulf Stream and leaving the last of the Bahamas behind us, the weather became more cool and the ocean less turbulent but with an incessant wind "dead ahead". As we approached still further northward there was a considerable change in the atmosphere. The weather was for a day or two, uncomfortably cold. Many of the passengers wrapped in overcoats or blankets, were lounging about upon the quarterdeck during the day, basking themselves in the sun and bed clothing in the night

177

would have been agreeable in fact almost necessary. But our cots not being furnished with the necessary articles and those not having their own blankets had to sleep without any covering. Unfortunately I was among the latter class.

On the evening of the ninth day after leaving Aspinwall, out steamer's bow was headed up the Bay of New York, upon whose smooth waters we were now swiftly and gracefully gliding along., close in shore, along which were scattered many cottages, dwellings, and little villas, all of which had more of a home-like appearance than any I have seen for five long years.

It may be that my long confinement upon the ocean has rendered my feelings more susceptible to the beauty of this scenery that it would otherwise have been, but as I view them, at this distance, I experience a peculiar feeling which is like being at home.

As we advance up the bay and just as the sun is disappearing in the western sky, we have a distant view of the great Emporium to which all eyes are not turned. Some of its lofty spires and glittering domes could be seen at this distance from the steamer.

A dense cloud hangs over it like a burnished canopy of ever-changing hues. The main land and the islands around are smiling in the first mellow tints of their autumnal glory. Many vessels of various descriptions are plying to and fro on the bright bosom of the ample bay and the shore is girded with a forest of masts and spars, from which float ever waving streamers.

At even o'clock P.M. our steamer is at her mooring. All is bustle and confusion. The mate is hoarsely giving the order to "make fast" and the sailors in obedience, are busy with the ropes and cables. The wharf is crowded with people and the weary voyagers are collecting their valuables and are preparing to bid the good steamer a joyful farewell.

Crowds of citizens are pressing their way on board in search of friends. Commotion and excitement rule the hour. Happy greetings, kind salutations, and smiling faces, indicate more strongly than words could express, the general joy that the voyage with its perils and pleasures was ended. All the passengers except the one who died have landed in safety and comfortable health.

The time since we left San Francisco is twenty-four and a half days and the length of our track according to the steamer reckoning is five thousand three hundred and fifteen (5315) miles.

On reaching the wharf, as may be expected on such occasions, we were surrounded by a whole bevy of runners and representatives of numerous hotels, offering us passage in their hacks or cabs free—gratis—for nothing and at the same time taking hold of some of the persons to drag them to their vehicles, which invitation was rather roughly rejected, with the accompaniment of some hard languages, by some of the party.

They intimated to us that we should remember that we are in a civilized country and not in California. We told them that we had hoped as much, but could not see much civility among this crew.

Six or eight of us passed on through the crowd of people and made our way uptown traversing various streets till we reached Courtland Street. Here we stopped in at a second-class hotel at which place we were accommodated with supper, lodging and breakfast. Our appearance at this time was not very presentable, as most of us had on their miner's duds. We have done ample justice to our supper which was more homelike than anything that we have had for many a day. And for the first time, on this occasion, since I left the States nearly five years ago, I slept upon a feather bed.

On the following morning after breakfast, a number of us sallied forth to a clothing store at which place transformation in regard to our clothing took place. Here we were all more or less fleeced out of several dollars. From this place we went to a bath room, where we had a general scrubbing from head to foot. This done, we went to a barber shop, from which we came forth with smooth faces, and closely cropped heads. By this time we presented a more respectable appearance.

After dinner, in company with several of my companions, I took a stroll about town to while away the time. At five o'clock P.M. I took the train to Philadelphia. Not one of my five hundred companions, who landed with me here not twenty-four hours ago, is present. All are scattered abroad and I am a stranger amidst hundreds of fellow travelers.

In due time we reached the Quaker City where I laid over for several hours, when I took the night train for Lancaster, at which place I arrived at two o'clock in the morning. Here for the balance of the morning, I took lodgings at the Railroad House, where I slept and rested till breakfast time.

After which, I went about town being market day, I expected to meet with some of my friends from the country but a heavy rain during the night set in which is still continuing and has caused rather a slim attendance at market. Not meeting with anyone with whom I am acquainted, at nine o'clock A.M. the rain having abated, I took the stage for Manheim, where after a few hours ride I arrived at twelve o'clock noon, in my old home and among numerous friends and old acquaintances.

Chapter 47
Some Unfathomable Transmigration

Here ends my wandering of five years, having left this place in October 1849 and traveled across the overland route to the Pacific Coast, thence returning by the ocean route to the Atlantic by which I was enabled to see much of this magnificent country.

The great rivers on the Pacific slope, with its fertile valleys and rich prairies which look up at the mountains and the mountains which look at on the sunset sea—these will give us the home standards of comparison which none but those who have made the transcontinental journey can form a veritable or intelligent view of the vastness of this country.

In the midst of the matchless energy and enterprise by which I have been surrounded during my sojourn of four years in California, I have sometimes imagined that the scenes in which I was moving were not enacted in the world in which I was born and reared, but that by some unfathomable transmigration I had become the subject of a new existence. Here virtue shines out too dimly in contrast with the dark deformity of over-shadowing, stalwart vice, faces, complexions, customs, habits, and business intercourse, manners, trade, laws, skies, air, earth, and all things so strange, so peculiar and unlike my old associations, that the doctrine of the ancient philosopher seemed at times plausible.

Wealth abound, but thousands are poor; labor is in demand, but troops of idles throng the streets and places of amusements. The necessaries of life are abundant. The advocates of temperance are active, but dram-drinking prevails to an elsewhere unheard of extent. The preacher of righteousness unceasingly lifts his voice, but the Sabbath desecration is almost universal, and gambling and licentiousness feels neither shame nor restraint. Criminal laws are stringent, and are enforced, but crimes of every grade are constantly perpetrated over the whole land.

And yet, despite these seeming inconsistencies, California is increasing in wealth, population, commercial influence, more rapidly than any other state in the Union.

I have been in many sections of the country, and have visited many cities and towns; have viewed with admiration its extensive plains, the principal rivers, the lofty mountain ranges, the snow clad Sierra Nevadas, and the hoary forests. I have mingled and toiled with the miners, in the midst of extensive and costly erections and operations.

I have enjoyed the cool embracing summer breezes of the Pacific Coast and endured the depressing influence of the interior climate, have seen heaps of gold and the mammoth productions of the soil, and wandered beneath the bright moon and stars, that illumine the inimitable evening sky.

And I have witnessed on the right hand and on the left, the rising as if by magic, dwellings, halls, warehouses and churches. In all this it is but just to say, that I have found much to approve and even admire.

I have formed many valuable acquaintances, with whom I should be happy to meet again and have enjoyed many social interviews, which will ever associate California with other cherished recollections of the past. Truly –

"There is a Divinity that shapes our ends, rough-hew them as we will."

I will now close my journal, and go and see how time has dealt with my old friends and acquaintances who I left behind me during my five years absence.

November 11*th*, 1854
D. B. Hackman

Chapter 48
Ere I Bid Farewell Forever

David informs his beloved Harriet that he has returned to Lancaster.

Lancaster
November 13ᵗʰ, 1854

Miss Miller,

Allow me to address you with a few lines to inform you that I have just returned from a short visit to Manheim, of which I have no doubt you are aware of. I regret to say that I have not had the honor of paying a visit to you. But as I had no one to introduce me to you, I was, for manners sake, obliged to leave Manheim even without seeing you. Knowing that there is a young man paying his respects to you, I do not wish to say much at present, but I wish to make one request of you which is that you will at least permit me to have one interview with you, ere I bid farewell forever. Indeed it would be most cruel of you to refuse me the request. Let me but see the image of my heart once more and I will never more intrude my presence upon you. I know not whether you still think anything of me or not, but that matters not or rather I leave that to yourself. I have yet one more request to make which is that you will please write me a few lines to Lancaster as soon as you receive this. I intend to return to Manheim in the course of a week or two when I should be happy to see you. But don't forget and write to me, no matter what you write. If you have anything against me, let me know it and if not let me know it also. But enough for the present.

I remain your humble admirer,

David B. Hackman

Chapter 49
Back in Manheim

According to the 1850 Census, Harriett Miller was the 21 year-old daughter of Adam and Rebecca Miller. She had a 29 year-old brother Richard. Adam was listed as a hatter, and the family lived in the borough of Manheim.

Harriett was amenable to David's advances. The courtship did not last very long. David Baer Hackman and Harriett B. Miller were married only six weeks after his return, on January 1, 1855. David and Harriett moved in with her parents and David was introduced to the hatters trade. Within a short time, a son, Augustus Miller Hackman, was born.

According to the 1860 Census, the Hackman–Miller household was comprised of Adam, David & Harriett, their son Augustus and a domestic, 17 year-old Adeline Staley. Rebecca Miller had passed away within the last year.

David's younger brother and frequent pen pal, Andrew, was 32 in 1860, and still a bachelor living with his mother, Anna Bear. Andrew would finally marry Martha Eschbach Brenner (1839-1916) at B Kauffman's tavern, soon after the outbreak of the Civil War, on September 5, 1861. Neither brother served for the Union. By 1870, Andrew and Martha were living on a farm in Warwick Township, with two daughters, Alice and Emma.

On April 22, 1864, David's business partner and father-in-law, Adam Miller, passed away. Sadly, Harriett also passed away, on December 9th 1870, leaving David a widower with his teen-aged son Augustus.

Circa 1875, David married Ellen Caroline Gabel, 25 years his junior. According to the 1880 Census, David had given up the hatter's trade to be a saloon keeper. He and "Ella" had three children: Franklin aged 4, Mabel aged 3, and Harry aged 1. Two boarders, involved in cigar making, also lived with them. Later that year, daughter Edith was born.

Since his departure for California, David never returned to the church. He had left his Mennonite roots and was now a saloon keeper, perhaps reminiscing of his California days. Imagine the stories he told across the bar about the days back in '49, when men from around the world flocked to California to seek their fortune!

Meanwhile, brother Andrew continued farming in Warwick township, and frequented the Church of the Brethren. By 1880, a son, Willis aged 3 (the author's great grandfather) was recorded.

Back in Manheim, on April 2nd, 1882, David's son Walter Scott Hackman was born. On May 1, 1885, David was still listed as an owner of an 'eating establishment' in Manheim. Not long after, on January 21st, 1886, his elderly mother, Susanna Frantz Bear Hackman Brubaker passed away.

Before David's passing on November 16th, 1896, there were records of his renting rooms to two Chinamen who wished to start a laundry (in 1894). He was also practicing as a boot & shoemaker on South Prussian (Main) Street in Manheim.

According to his obituary, David joined the Reformed Church just before his death. Perhaps he was reforming himself, in preparation!

In conclusion, the forty years David lived after his California adventure likely did not match the excitement of his youth. David changed trades several times and appeared to be involved in various small ventures around town. Perhaps he was the typical small-town entrepreneur, always 'just missing' the big win – just like he did in California.

Chapter 50
David Baer Hackman Time Line

Circa 1820 – 1st Cousin and Step-Sister Catherine H. Brubaker (Eberly) is born

Circa 1820 – 1st Cousin and Step-Sister Nancy Brubaker (Bennetch) is born

Circa 1820 – 1st Cousin and Step-Brother Henry H. Brubaker is born

Circa 1824 – Parents David Heistand Hackman and Susanna Frantz Baer marry

Circa 1825 – 1st Cousin and Step-Sister Elizabeth Brubaker (Eberly) is born

Mar 26th 1825 – Older brother Jacob Baer Hackman is born

Mar 19th 1827 – David Baer Hackman is born

Jul 5th 1828 – Younger brother Andrew Baer Hackman is born

Feb 5th 1829 – First Wife Harriet B. Miller is born

Nov 27th 1829 – Younger sister Anna Hackman is born

Apr 10th 1830 – Younger sister Anna Hackman dies at 5 months

Jun 28th 1831 – Uncle Henry Heistand Hackman dies

Nov 26th 1831 – Uncle John Gingrich dies in Waterloo, Canada

Dec 29th 1831 – Father David Heistand Hackman dies at age 30

Mar 10th 1832 – 1st Cousin and Step-Brother Jacob H Brubaker is born

Circa 1837 – Aunt Catherine Hackman Brubaker dies

Jun 16th 1837 – 1st Cousin and Step-Brother Jonas H Brubaker is born

Circa 1838 – Mother Susanna marries Uncle John Gesell Brubaker

Circa 1839 – Aunt Maria Baer Brubaker dies

Circa 1840 – Grandfather Jacob Brubaker Hackman dies

Aug 14th 1840 – Half-Sister Susan B. Brubaker is born

Jul 3rd 1843 – Half-Sister Fanny Brubaker is born

Circa 1844 – Half-Sister Mary Brubaker is born

1846 – A&C Miller, Hatters is at 11 South Prussian (Main) St., Manheim

Apr 25th 1846 – War with Mexico begins

Oct 25th 1846 – Half-Brother Isaac Brubaker is born

Sep 14th 1847 – Hostilities with Mexico cease when Mexico City is occupied

Jan 24th 1848 – Gold discovered at Sutter's Mill near Sacramento, CA

Feb 2nd 1848 – Peace Treaty signed with Mexico ceding the American Southwest

Jun 23rd 1849 – Aunt Maria Long (Snavely) Hackman dies

Winter 1849-1850 – David is in Ohio (ending in Delaware, OH)

Circa 1850 – Grandmother Anna Frantz Baer dies at age 71

Mar 1850 – David joins company traveling to California from Delaware, OH

Apr 1st 1850 – David and company leave Delaware, OH

Apr 5th 1850 – David reaches Cincinnati, OH

Apr 6th 1850 – David leaves Cincinnati, OH

Apr 12th 1850 – David is in St. Louis, MO

Apr 19th 1850 – David arrives on the shore of the Missouri River

Apr 21st 1850 – David writes mother from the Missouri River near Independence

Apr 21st 1850 – David writes brother Andrew from St. Joseph, MO

May 5th 1850 – The company crosses the Missouri River and heads West

July 9th 1850 – President Zachary Taylor dies – succeeded by Millard Fillmore

Aug 1850 – Following the Humboldt River

Aug 25th 1850 – David arrives in California – crossing took 112 days

Sep 9th 1850 – California becomes the 31st state

Nov 7th 1850 – David writes Andrew from Hangtown, California

Nov 8th 1850 – David writes Harriet from Hangtown, California

Dec 4th 1850 – (approx.) Hanging of Dick Crone

Dec 11th 1850 – (approx.) Friend Mr. Kline returning to "States"

Dec 12th 1850 – (approx.) David & Mr. Kline in Sacramento City

Dec 19th 1850 - Census lists David "Heckman" in Placerville, El Dorado County

Dec 25th 1850 – David writes from Hangtown, California

1851 – Gold discovered at Greenhorn Creek, Kern Co, CA

Apr 26th 1851 – 2nd Wife Ellen Caroline Gabel is born

1852 - Hydraulic mining began at American Hill just north of Nevada City

1852 – Hydraulic mining at Yankee Jims in Placer County.

Mar 5th 1852 – David writes Andrew from Mokelumna Hill, CA

Nov 24th 1852 – David writes Andrew from Columbia, CA

1853 – First extensive underground mining at Forest Hill District, CA

1853 – Gold found at Columbia, Tuolumne Co, CA

1853 – Franklin Pierce inaugurated as President

May 29th 1853 – David writes Andrew from Yankee Hill, CA

Oct 4th 1854 – David writes Harriet from Columbia, CA

Nov 11th 1854 – David is back in Manheim, PA

Nov 19th 1854 – David writes Harriet from Lancaster, PA

Jan 1st 1855 – Marries Harriet B. Miller in Manheim, PA

Circa 1856 – Son Augustus Miller Hackman is born

Mar 1857 – James Buchanan of Lancaster, PA becomes President

Sep 13th 1857 – 3rd Cousin Once Removed Milton Snavely Hershey is born

Circa 1858 – Uncle Isaac F. Baer dies

Circa 1859 – Mother-in-Law Rebecca Miller dies

Jun 12 1860 – 1860 Census – living with wife & FIL Adam Miller the hatter

Aug 18th 1860 – Half-Sister Susan B. Brubaker dies at age 20

Circa 1861 – 1st Cousin and Step-Sister Elizabeth Brubaker Eberly dies

Mar 1861 – Abraham Lincoln is inaugurated to succeed Buchanan

Apr 12th 1861 – Confederates fire on Fort Sumter to start Civil War

Sep 5th 1861 – Brother Andrew marries Martha Eschbach Brenner

Nov 21st 1862 – Aunt Anna Hackman Gingrich dies in Canada

Jun 27th 1863 – Carlisle, PA captured by the Confederates

Jun 28th 1863 – Columbia-Wrightsville Bridge burned by Union to deter Rebels

Jul 1st -3rd 1863 – Battle of Gettysburg

Apr 22nd 1864 – Father-in-Law Adam Miller dies

Aug 24th 1867 – Half-Brother Isaac Brubaker dies at age 20

Mar 11th 1869 – Charter Member of the Selah Lodge No. 657 I.O.O.F.

Jul 27th 1870 – Census – David is listed as a Hatter w/wife & Augustus

Dec 9th 1870 – Wife Harriet B. Miller Hackman dies

Apr 26th 1873 – 1st Cousin and Step-Brother Jacob H. Brubaker dies

Circa 1875 – Marries Ellen Caroline Gabel Hackman

Aug 20th 1875 – Son Franklin Gabel Hackman is born

Circa 1877 – Daughter Mabel E. Hackman (Radcliff) is born

Feb 21st 1877 – Nephew Willis Brenner Hackman is born (Andrew's son)

Circa 1878 – Grandson Charles B. Hackman is born (Augustus's son)

May 10th 1878 – David is listed as running an eating establishment in Manheim

Sep 23rd 1878 – Son Harry Baer Hackman is born

Circa 1880 – Daughter Edith Hackman is born

Jun 5th 1880 – 1880 Census – David listed as a saloon keeper

Apr 12th 1882 – Son Walter Scott Hackman is born

Feb 27th 1884 – Step-Father and Uncle John Gesell Brubaker dies

May 1 1885 – David still owns and operates an eating establishment

Jun 18th 1885 – Aunt Veronica Baer dies

Jan 21st 1886 – Mother Susanna Frantz Baer Hackman Brubaker dies

Mar 9th 1887 – 1st Cousin and Step-Brother Jonas H.
 Brubaker dies
May 25 1894 – Rents rooms to two Chinamen who wish to
 start a laundry
1896 – David is a Boot & Shoemaker on South Prussian
 (Main) St.
Nov 16th 1896 – David Baer Hackman dies
May 9th 1897 – Sister-in-Law Maria Hackman dies (wife of
 Jacob)
Jan 20th 1899 – Brother Jacob Baer Hackman dies
Jun 7th 1900 – 1900 Census – Ellen, Harry & Walter live at
 133 South Charlotte St.
Nov 23rd 1901 – Father-in-Law's Brother Harry Miller dies
Aug 8th 1903 – Grandson Frank Metger Hackman is born
 (son of Franklin)
Oct 28th 1906 – Brother-in-Law Benjamin Bollinger dies
Feb 22nd 1907 – 2nd Wife Ellen Caroline Gabel Hackman
 dies
Jul 17th 1913 – Sister-in-Law Martha Eschbach Brenner
 Hackman dies
Jul 17th 1916 – Brother Andrew Baer Hackman dies
Feb 22nd 1931 – Son Harry Baer Hackman dies
Aug 16th 1935 – Half-Sister Fanny Brubaker Bollinger dies

About the Author

Lawrence Knorr is the 2nd great grand nephew of David Baer Hackman. The letters written by David to his brother were written to Lawrence's 2nd great grandfather Andrew Baer Hackman.

Lawrence is the author of several other books including *The Relations of Milton Snavely Hershey, The Hackman Story* (with cousin Dorothy Elaine Grace), *The Descendants of Hans Peter Knorr, General John Fulton Reynolds: His Biography, Words and Relations* (with Michael Riley and Diane Watson), *The Relations of Isaac F. Stiely: Minister of the Mahantongo Valley,* and *The Relations of Dwight D. Eisenhower.*

Lawrence is the father of two beautiful daughters, Taylor and Abbey, and resides near Harrisburg, PA with his wife Tammi. Professionally, he is the Director of Strategic Integration for Ahold USA (the grocery chain) and was the Chief Information Officer for the Pennsylvania Liquor Control Board. He is also an accomplished graphic artist.

Lawrence holds a Bachelors Degree in Business & Economics (History Minor) from Wilson College and a Masters of Business Administration from the Pennsylvania State University. He is also a Project Management

Professional and Certified Computer Professional. Lawrence also teaches part-time as an adjunct professor at Harrisburg University.

David Hackman's story was discovered in the archives of the Lancaster County Historical Society. Lawrence also followed David's footsteps in the gold fields of California, visiting the towns he lived and worked in.

"Through his journal and letters, Uncle David passed on an incredible tale—one that captured my imagination. Few have written of their Gold Rush adventure as well as David – a very astute observer. My only wish is that it was longer so that I might continue this labor of love!"

Made in the USA
Monee, IL
07 July 2026

56544764R00114